Post-growth Economics and Society

We stand on the threshold of a "post-growth" world – one in which the relentless pursuit of economic growth has ceased to constitute a credible societal project. The symptoms that mark the end of an era are clear and incontrovertible: a return to the regularities of the past is illusory. The pursuit of economic growth no longer constitutes a credible societal project for ecological, social and geopolitical reasons.

Edited by and written by a wide range of scholars, this book identifies several areas in which we must fundamentally rethink our societal organization. They ask what it means to abandon the objective of economic growth; how we can encourage the emergence of other visions to guide society; how global visions and local transition initiatives should be connected; which modes of governance should be associated with the required social and technological innovations. Alongside the necessary respect of ecological limits and equity in distribution, the promotion of autonomy (involving all in the building of socio-political norms) could serve for guidance. The topics addressed over the chapters range from the future of work to the decommodification of economic relations; the search for new indicators of progress to decentralized modes of governance; and from the circular economy to polycentric transitions. Each contribution brings a unique perspective, a piece of a larger puzzle to be assembled.

Post-growth Economics and Society is an important volume to those who study ecological economics, political economy and the environment and society. It invites theorists as much as practitioners to re-explore the roots of our societal goals and play an active role in the systemic shift to come.

Isabelle Cassiers is Professor at the University of Louvain, Belgium, Senior Researcher at the Belgian Fund for Scientific Research and member of the Royal Academy of Belgium.

Kevin Maréchal is Associate Professor at Gembloux Agro Bio Tech/University of Liège, invited lecturer at the University of Louvain and Senior Researcher at CESSE-ULB, Belgium.

Dominique Méda is Professor at Paris-Dauphine University, Director of the Institute of Interdisciplinary Studies in Social Sciences (IRISSO) and Head of the Chair "Ecological Conversion, Work, Employment, Social Policies" at the College of Global Studies, France.

Routledge Studies in Ecological Economics

For a full list of titles in this series, please visit www.routledge.com/series/RSEE

Post-growth Economics and Society

Exploring the Paths of a Social and Ecological Transition

**Edited by
Isabelle Cassiers,
Kevin Maréchal and
Dominique Méda**

Routledge
Taylor & Francis Group

LONDON AND NEW YORK

First published 2018 by Routledge

2 Park Square, Milton Park, Abingdon, Oxfordshire OX14 4RN

52 Vanderbilt Avenue, New York, NY 10017

Routledge is an imprint of the Taylor & Francis Group, an informa business

First issued in paperback 2019

British Library Cataloguing in Publication Data
A catalogue record for this book is available from the British Library

Library of Congress Cataloging in Publication Data
A catalog record for this book has been requested

ISBN: 978-1-138-50327-4 (hbk)
ISBN: 978-0-367-34047-6 (pbk)

Typeset in Times New Roman
by Wearset Ltd, Boldon, Tyne and Wear

Contents

Contributors

Thomas Bauwens, PhD in Economics. Post-doctoral fellow at the Swiss Federal Institute of Technology in Lausanne (EPFL). Research on the economics of collective action and its applications in the field of sustainable energy innovations. Author of several scientific publications in international journals on these topics. More detail on www.researchgate.net/profile/Thomas_Bauwens.

Isabelle Cassiers (co-editor of the book), Professor in Economics at the University of Louvain (UCL, Belgium) and Senior Researcher at the Belgian Fund for Scientific Research. Member of the Royal Academy of Belgium. For thirty years (1975–2005), her scientific research, rooted in regulation theory, has been dedicated to economic and social history. Her historical researches have convinced her of the urgent need for an interdisciplinary reflection on the theme of redefining prosperity (Routledge 2015, first published in French by Editions de l'Aube, 2011 and 2013), to which she has devoted herself since 2006, with particular focus on the issue of "beyond GDP" indicators. More on www.isabellecassiers.be.

Olivier De Schutter, Professor at the University of Louvain (UCL) and at SciencesPo (Paris). He holds a LLM from Harvard University, and a PhD in Law from the University of Louvain. He was a visiting professor at Columbia University in the years 2008–2013 and, in 2013–2014, he was a visiting professor at UC Berkeley, where he helped launch the Berkeley Food Institute. Specialized in economic and social rights, De Schutter was the United Nations Special Rapporteur on the Right to Food between 2008 and 2014, and since 2015 he is a member of the UN Committee on Economic, Social and Cultural Rights. He co-chairs the International Panel of Experts on Sustainable Food Systems (IPES-Food). He was awarded the prestigious Francqui Prize in 2013 for his contribution to international and European human rights law and to the theory of governance.

Stephan Kampelmann, economist. Researcher at the Laboratory for Urbanism, Infrastructure and Ecology (LoUIsE), Faculty of Architecture La Cambre-Horta, University of Brussels (ULB). His academic work focuses on questions related to socio-economic inequalities and urban ecology and has been published in journals such as *Socio-Economic Review*, the *British Journal of Industrial Relations* and *Ecological Economics*. Stephan Kampelmann is founding member of the Urban Ecology Centre (Brussels) and OSMOS (Stuttgart), a spin-off company providing services in the field of participatory planning. Personal websites: www.urban-ecology.be and www.osmosnetwork.com.

Kevin Maréchal (co-editor of the book), Associate Professor at Gembloux Agro Bio Tech/University of Liège and invited lecturer at the University of Louvain (UCL). Senior researcher and member of the executive committee of the Centre for Economic and Social Studies on the Environment (CESSE-ULB). Grounded in a reflection on the change of climate in economics (Routledge, 2012), he has carried out several researches on the issue of socio-technical and behavioural lock-in (in various sectors such as climate, energy and food). These researches have been published in scientific journals (e.g. *Ecological Economics*, *Energy Policy*, etc.). Details on http://dev.ulb.ac.be/ceese/CEESE/en/staff.php?menu=2&profil=78.

Dominique Méda (co-editor of the book), sociologist and philosopher. Professor at Paris-Dauphine University, PSL Research University. Director of the Institute of Interdisciplinary Studies in Social Sciences (IRISSO). Head of the Chair "Ecological Conversion, Work, Employment, Social Policies" at the College of Global Studies (FMSH). She has published several books on the issue of growth where she proposes a critical appraisal of its merits. Details on http://irisso.dauphine.fr/fileadmin/mediatheque/irisso/documents/CVMe__damai2016.doc-1.pdf.

Sybille Mertens, PhD in Economics. Associate Professor at University of Liège. Holder of the Cera Chair in Cooperative and Social Entrepreneurship. Member of the Centre for Social Economy (HEC-Liège). Research interests: non-capitalist firms (with a focus on their business models and on social impact assessment tools). Publications record is available on www.ces.ulg.ac.be/en_GB/about-ces/team/sybille-mertens-2.

Bernard Perret, engineer and socio-economist. Has achieved a double career of civil servant and social scientist. Member of the general inspectorate of the French ministry of ecology until 2016, now retired. Member of the editorial committee of several publications, including *Esprit, Projet et Evaluation* (published in London), commentator in daily newspaper *La Croix*. Lecturer at the Paris Catholic Institute. Main books: *L'économie contre la société* (with Guy Roustang, Seuil, 1993), *La logique de l'espérance* (Presses de la Renaissance, 2006), *Pour une raison écologique* (Flammarion, 2011), *L'évaluation des politiques publiques* (La Découverte, 2001, 2008, 2014) and *Au-delà du marché, les nouvelles voies de la démarchandisation* (Les petits matins, 2015).

Géraldine Thiry, master degrees in political sciences and in economics, and PhD in economics (University of Louvain – UCL). She is Associate Professor at ICHEC Brussels Management School and invited associate professor at the University of Louvain (UCL). Her research focuses on new indicators beyond GDP, socio-economics of quantification, ecological economics and the poverty–environment nexus (see www.geraldinethiry.be). In 2016 she was research consultant for the Oxford Poverty and Human Development Initiative (OPHI) and worked on integrating environmental and natural resources within the multidimensional poverty index (MPI).

Acknowledgements

This book began with the project, originally entrusted to Isabelle Cassiers, who was then immediately joined by Kevin Maréchal, of devising and directing a committee on *post-growth* for the 21st Congress of French-speaking Belgian economists, "Growth: realities and perspectives". The two surrounded themselves with the contributing authors of this volume, for the most part economists, taking care to enrich the discussion with contributions from other disciplines, such as sociology and philosophy (with co-editor Dominique Méda), or governance theory (with Olivier De Schutter), all the while attempting to keep the gender balance equal. The authors met prior to the congress to discuss the first version of their texts. They benefited on this occasion from the constructive comments and suggestions of eight readers to whom they wish to express their thanks: Paul-Marie Boulanger (IDD), Laurent de Briey (UNamur), Bruno Kestemont (Statbel), Eloi Laurent (OFCE/Science Po and Stanford University), Jérôme Pelenc (ULB), Anaïs Perilleux (UCL), Edgar Szoc (Haute école Paul-Henri Spaak) and Pascale Vielle (UCL). They also wish to extend their gratitude to the congress president, Eric De Keuleneer, for the initial invitation; to his General Secretary, Abdelfattah Touzri, for his endless patience and his help with the redaction of the texts; to the Institut d'analyse du changement dans l'histoire et les sociétés contemporaines (IACCHOS-UCL) for their financial support; as well as to Coralie Muylaert for her help at the final stage. This volume was first published in French by Les éditions de l'Aube in 2017 with the title *Vers une société post-croissance – Intégrer les défis écologiques, économiques et sociaux*. We wish to thank the anonymous referees who supported the project for publication and the translators who assisted us in bringing it to English. Very warm thanks to all those who have contributed to making this book a reality.

1 The economy in a post-growth era

What project and what philosophy?

Isabelle Cassiers and Kevin Maréchal

If the earth must lose that great portion of its pleasantness which it owes to things that the unlimited increase of wealth and population would extirpate from it, for the mere purpose of enabling it to support a larger, but not a better or a happier population, I sincerely hope, for the sake of posterity, that they will be content to be stationary, long before necessity compels them to it.

It is scarcely necessary to remark that a stationary condition of capital and population implies no stationary state of human improvement. There would be as much scope as ever for all kinds of mental culture, and moral and social progress; as much room for improving the Art of Living, and much more likelihood of its being improved, when minds ceased to be engrossed by the art of getting on.

(John Stuart Mill 1848)

Since the beginning of our discipline, economists have confronted questions about values, goals, the distribution of wealth and the limits imposed by nature. The thoughts of the founding fathers, often steeped in philosophy, were marked by the emergence of the industrial age and by the upheaval it brought to the traditional societies of the time. Everything suggests that we are once more at a major historical turning point. The unprecedented ecological and geopolitical challenges that we face are forcing economists to revisit the seminal questions of their discipline.

Improving the Art of Living without being obsessed by the art of getting on, accepting the idea of reaching a "stationary condition of capital and population" without renouncing human improvement, is there any more current programme or more pertinent question? At the point at which humanity finds itself, exploring the realities and perspectives of economic growth *inevitably* leads to thinking of post-growth.[1] This claim, which may seem strong, is shared by the authors brought together in this book. Each of them brings a specific point of view, a piece of the jigsaw puzzle that will have to be assembled in the future. Starting from the double meaning of the French word "*Economie*", we treat here both the economy as a social system ("the state of a country or region in terms of the production and consumption of goods and services and the supply of money", *Oxford Living Dictionaries*) and the particular discipline of economics. Together, and without claiming to have covered the entirety of themes that should ideally be explored, we have unravelled a thread that we will retrace in this introductory chapter.[2] We proceed in four steps:

1   What should be understood by the term "post-growth"?
2   What are the major problems that arise when one abandons the objective of continuous growth?
3   How can we make the transition to another horizon?
4   What are the models of thought and modes of government most likely to bring about a coherent project?

A post-growth era

The term "post-growth" signifies a *beyond*, an era that we are entering and yet are unable to define precisely, other than by reference to what we are leaving behind.[3] The symbols that signal the end of an epoch are sufficiently numerous and clear that any thought of a return to past norms is an illusion. Yet the unique historical nature and complexity of the situation are such that we can only fumble our way forward.

What we call "post-growth" is not a crisis (a temporary status before a return to normality), nor is it an incurred deceleration of economic activity (a situation that we have been in, de facto, for several decades); it is not even a secular stagnation (the hypothesis mainly discussed by economists these days). By post-growth we mean *an era in which the societal project is redefined beyond the pursuit of economic growth.*[4] Breaking from such a pursuit strikes us as essential and urgent for many reasons.

First, considering the situation in Europe, it seems very likely that anaemic growth will persist in the medium term.[5] Moreover, Maddison (2001) observes that at the secular scale, a rate of economic growth above one per cent is a recent phenomenon and the rates recorded in the West during the post-war decades are an historical exception. In these conditions, remaining besotted with growth is both unproductive and hopeless. Unproductive, because vast reserves of energy are sacrificed to a lost cause. Hopeless, because the promises made to populations – most notably of full employment – are repeatedly broken. This feeds a growing distrust of the political class and can bring populist parties to power, with their simplistic and seductive rhetoric. The sociopolitical dangers of such a situation alone are a sufficiently compelling reason to abandon the objective of sustained growth, an objective whose realization is, in any case, improbable.

More fundamentally, even if it were possible for our economies to recover such growth, the ensuing disadvantages would undoubtedly outweigh the expected benefits. Numerous studies (we mention, among others, Méda 2008, 2013; Jackson 2009, 2017; Costanza *et al.* 2012; Cassiers 2015) recall, update and reinforce the now ancient diagnosis about "The Limits to Growth" (Meadows *et al.* 1972) and the proposition to "Free the future" (Illich 1971).[6]

The most obvious damaging effects are ecological. On this point, doubt is no longer possible (Steffen *et al.* 2015). Our generation lives at the cost of those that follow. The ecosystem cannot support the current rate of human activity and it is urgent that we break from this trend; every delay serves only to exacerbate the problem. Of course, *one part* of the response to this challenge must lie in technological innovation aimed at a radical decoupling of the production of goods and services from their ecological impact (consumption of material resources and pollution). However, betting purely on technology would be irresponsible since nothing guarantees inventions of sufficient magnitude (both in terms of innovation and implementation). The *other part* of the response must therefore consist in changing our way of life – just as radically. Given the large gap in wealth between the countries in the global North and South, it is clear that the most serious efforts must be made by the wealthier countries, whether for ethical considerations or simply out of geopolitical prudence.

Independent of ecological limits, it should be noted that the main benefits formerly attributed to growth have largely faded over time, at least within wealthy countries. This is particularly the case of reduced inequality and increased welfare of populations. While growth in the post-war boom (1945–1975) led to income and wealth being shared more equitably, that of the following decades (and in particular of the last thirty years) has indeed been accompanied by a dramatic increase in inequality, highlighted by numerous studies, most notably by Wilkinson and Pickett (2009), the OECD (2011) and Piketty (2014). The myth that the enrichment of the wealthiest would "trickle down" to the lower classes of the social pyramid now appears to be dispelled.

The question of the link between growth and well-being deserves careful consideration. There is no denying that material progress has lifted much of mankind out of poverty. But we must also recognize that the values to which an affluent middle-class population attaches the greatest importance (social ties, health, participation in civic society, quality of life, etc.) are *not* correlated with growth and are often threatened by its adverse side effects (Easterlin 1974; Cassiers and Delain 2006, among others). Moreover, our societies have created a type of addiction to growth with its set of alienating effects (Arnsperger 2005; Jackson 2009, 2017). It is our relation to this "cage" that Olivier De Schutter discusses in his contribution to this book, before examining ways of breaking free from it.

To summarize, our thoughts on post-growth begin with an observation: growth has been thoroughly exhausted as a social project (Laurent 2017). Now, the pressing task is to contribute – even if only by providing markers for general guidance – to the emergence of an alternative project capable of supporting essential human values while also respecting the limits of our planet.

The challenges to overcome

Renouncing the objective of growth is clearly not easy: the social contracts made in the period after the Second World War were explicitly sealed with this common goal, which made it possible to overcome the obstacles arising from the many social conflicts of the time. While regulation has changed profoundly between the post-war boom (1945–1975) and the decades that followed, governments – as well as most other social actors – continue to behave as if programmed for the continued pursuit of growth.

This addiction to growth likely springs from the difficulty of conceiving new ways to respond to core economic questions: the distribution of income while limiting social tensions; the creation of jobs to compensate for those destroyed by structural changes and technological progress; the provision of sufficient public funds to cover the costs of services and social security; the contribution to economic dynamism (innovation, entrepreneurship); the maintaining of a respected position, as a region or as a country, in the world economy, and thus remaining a loud voice in the concert of nations.

Answers to these questions are of two types. First, the work of Demailly *et al.* (2013), based on current empirical data, shows the increased importance of policy in a low-growth regime: if such regimes are to remain compatible with a reduction of inequality and a high level of social security, they must explicitly place much more importance on questions of distribution. "Ultimately, without a 'bubble of oxygen' from growth, we need more reforms, more political action" (Demailly *et al.* 2013: 66).

Second, and undoubtedly more fundamentally, these questions should be traced back to their roots and compared with overall societal goals. Is it necessary to create jobs, or should we seek, rather, to ensure that every citizen has the possibility to hold a dignified role in society and benefit from a quality of life that is both materially and culturally decent? Must we perpetually aim for productivity gains or should we now focus on gains in quality, as Dominique Méda suggests elsewhere in this volume? Is income the primary route to a good life, or can we break the alienating consumerist spiral and increase our happiness via the many *new paths of decommodification*, as Bernard Perret suggests? Does the dynamism of the economy necessarily rely on the lure of profit and permanent increases in income, or can we find in the social economy (see the contribution by Thomas Bauwens and Sybille Mertens) the beginnings of another logic that is no less dynamic and capable of spreading more widely? In a time of worldwide ecological crisis, does our place in the concert of nations truly depend on our commercial competitiveness or on our desire to maintain our fundamental values?

The transition towards a post-growth economy inevitably poses a series of fundamental questions that force us to reconsider the very essence of our economic model. Obviously, this may be unsettling. Where and how are we supposed to advance if our final destination and means of getting there are unknown? To attempt to respond to this, we appeal to the chain of thought espoused by André Gorz (1980) and Cornélius Castoriadis (1998) who, from the end of the post-war boom, situated radical change (in its etymological sense of "at the roots") in our logic of evolution, not in the definition of a coherent political project but rather in the subversion by the imaginary.

The various contributions in this book emphasize the importance of collectively thinking out this subversive imaginary in order for it to become a unifying element. This requires first and foremost the confrontation of inequality. As Gadrey (2014: 7, our translation) says, "the ecological transition will be social or it will not happen at all. Its acceptability depends on its ability to benefit everyone. Otherwise, it will be rejected as an additional factor of injustice".

The sheer novelty of a new imaginary attitude – the necessary rupture with the status quo – might seem paralysing or impossibly utopian, but Bernard Perret reminds us that a growing number of citizens are already putting this imagination into practice on a daily basis. This transition, the movement towards the beyond, is undoubtedly afoot:

> For about ten years, individuals and groups tired of changing only according to technological and economic imperatives have been declaring themselves to be "in transition", showing that their concerns reach beyond the present and that they even know which destination to aim for.
>
> (Chabot 2015: 19, our translation)

The paths of transition: cultivating the in-between

Although the system in which we operate is still largely dominated by the imperative of growth, the paths of transition towards deliberate (as opposed to enforced) post-growth are open.[7] The signs are clear. The fact that many actors are already mapping out these paths shows that it is not an unattainable utopia. Historians of economic and social development – in particular, historians of the long-term, such as Fernand Braudel (1977) – remind us how historically unprecedented systems have emerged very gradually from preceding socio-economic structures and how the old and the new co-exist for decades until the logic of the new prevails. Those parts of our discipline that have integrated fine historical analysis into their research methods, such as the regulation school (Boyer and Saillard 2002), show that transitions always involve a phase of hybridization. From this point of view, what appears as a crisis to contemporary eyes will be seen as a social laboratory by those who read the history *a posteriori*. The current challenge is to accelerate the structuration (in a coherent and well-articulated manner) of those initiatives already in place which partially answer the ecological and social problems of our times.

The "Transition Towns" movement, an intrinsically citizen-led and decentralized movement launched by Rob Hopkins (2008), is emblematic of the emergence of alternative ways of working, producing, consuming, exchanging, moving, protecting oneself from dangers, building relationships, finding a place in society, and feeling responsible and integrated. The overarching motive here is resilience. Pascal Chabot observes that

> the method used to extricate oneself from present difficulties is "visualization", a sort of imagination of a possible and desirable future that will serve as a guiding ideal for individual and collective actions [...] Pragmatism is the rule, and if there is indeed a reflexion that one could call down-to-earth, it is this.
>
> (Chabot 2015: 24, our translation)

This same pragmatism inspires various grassroots initiatives driven by actors with diverse profiles who attempt to act, at their scale, in accordance with their visions of the world. We mention, without claiming to be exhaustive, local purchasing groups and other short (food) supply chains bringing consumers closer to producers while sensitising them to social and environmental ethics; complementary currencies which combine a local means of payment with the defence of specific values or the support of a particular community; urban collective gardens and permaculture as a social movement; various forms of sharing economy, from carpooling to couch-surfing; the functional economy, in which the acquisition of products is replaced by access to the services rendered by these products, thereby encouraging robustness and durability, and eventually reducing the need for their production; and the social economy in its various forms for which profit is not an end.

The rise of initiatives such as these illuminates new zones of action, overtaking the traditional oppositions between state and market, private and public, profit and non-profit. The analytic and conceptual complexity of what we might be tempted to call an *in-between* seems to us to cover much larger ground. The different contributions to this book bear witness to this in that they explore the bypassing of dichotomies that, while often used to structure debate, can prove restrictive or even sclerotic when it comes to envisaging what is at stake in a post-growth era. The idea of a polycentric transition, developed by Thomas Bauwens and Sybille Mertens and also discussed in Stephan Kampelmann's empirical study, suggests the fecundity of an *in-between* that would break the traditional oppositions of *bottom-up* and *top-down*, of centralized and decentralized management. Fully grasping the dynamics of this *in-between* thus appears crucial to adequately apprehend the ecological and social transition.

In this regard, the notion of *autonomy* seems essential. The actors who are already tracing the broad lines of the post-growth era have not typically waited for orders from on high, and even less for the elaboration of an exhaustive project. On the contrary, they have often opted for the pragmatic route (for some, after having been disappointed by the failure of more global perspectives: sustainable development policy at the level of the United Nations, involvement in politics or in unions). This observation leads us back to the great thinkers in political ecology, such as André Gorz and Ivan Illich, who sought to promote the autonomy of individuals, as opposed to a paralysing heteronomy.[8] For these authors, autonomy is to be deployed at the heart of a collective, where interactions take place on a basis of reciprocity and solidarity. One can speak of an *autonomous sphere*, this *in-between* situated between the private and public spheres and which is currently shaping the contours of a different economic model that is social, collaborative, in transition, and decommodified in nature.

The ecological challenge requires a transformation of the social organization which can only be undertaken if it is conceived and carried out by individuals themselves, rather than dictated by an "expertocratic"[9] will to proceed to an ecological modernization of productive capacities. The autonomous sphere brings about a transformation of the relationship of citizens to diverse dimensions of economic life: work, consumption, production, exchange, etc. Dominique Méda's analysis points to the need for a better distribution among the population of the heteronomous work (that spent for a third party) so as to increase the amount of time dedicated to activities that are autonomously determined, the latter leaving more room for creativity.

Bearing in mind that the possibilities of creation and adaptability to change are key elements for the resilience of ecosystems, Gerber (2013: 40, cited in Rasteau 2015, our translation) establishes an interesting parallel between the fragility of monocultures and that of human beings subjected to forced industrialization: the standardization and automation of production processes often renders them too homogenous and passive; hence they "become more fragile socially and intellectually but also as a species capable of self-organising and facing up to challenges". Conversely, permaculture, as farming practice and philosophy, revitalizes both the earth and living beings, as well as restoring their creative potential.

How best to encourage citizens in transition to reach a critical mass (Arnsperger 2015), how best to enable an *autonomous sphere* to lead to a systemic change? Once again, the idea of an *in-between* seems fruitful. Is it not between the bottom-up and the top-down, and between local experimentation and global visualization, that we should think of a well-articulated connection?

A coherent framework of thought for a polycentric governance

If a systematic exploration of the *in-between* (beginning with the recognition of its existence) is necessary for a good understanding of what is at stake in post-growth, then we must find an analytic framework compatible with its dialectic investigation.

In the path opened by Thorstein Veblen (1898), over a hundred years ago, we formulate the following hypothesis, which is given in more detail in preceding works (Maréchal 2012): the standard model in economics has great difficulty accounting for the richness of the *in-between* because it is not evolutionary. By this, we mean the fact of relying on an originally Darwinian understanding of change and on the related analysis of economic systems as complex adaptive systems. Accordingly, it would surely be productive for economics to break free from the mechanistic logic borrowed from Newtonian physics and instead to explore biological metaphors or, more broadly, to find inspiration in living processes. Much research in economics is already exploring such paths. In the first instance, we could think of the theoretical developments in *evolutionary economics* and *ecological economics*. We could also mention how the logic of living processes has given rise to a range of more applied concepts such as industrial ecology, biomimicry and circular economy (the latter is explored by Stephan Kampelmann in his contribution). Some of the core concepts of the evolutionary paradigm, such as resilience, dynamic interdependencies, diversity and emergent properties, are now used to characterize and analyse themes which are incontestably economic and essential for understanding post-growth, such as the complexity and stability of monetary systems (Lietaer *et al.* 2010). Other fertile routes for analysing this transition are now sanctified by our profession: the attribution of the Nobel Prize in economics to Elinor Ostrom, economist *and* political scientist, for her empirical work on collective action and government of common goods, is a legitimization of the scientific interest residing in the exploration of the in-between.

Yet more fundamentally, as is proposed by *Social Ecological Economics* and is underlined by Géraldine Thiry in her contribution, it seems essential that in the future our discipline accepts the challenge of questioning not only its methods, but also its epistemology, its ethics, right up to its ontology. Confronted by serious ecological threats and the related radical uncertainty, only a reflexive posture will allow economists to take part in the development of Sustainability Science (Dedeurwaerdere 2014).

An evolution in this sense of economic theory, and more generally in the discourse which dominates economics, would greatly facilitate the governance of post-growth. Let us observe that there are multiple suggestions for other *foundations* on which to build a well-articulated connection between economic analysis and governance. They emanate from diverse and often unexpected communities that propose – in the form of reports, manifestos or even encyclicals – *a new development paradigm* (NDPSCS 2013), *a convivial society*,[10] *new economic principles* (NEF 2015), or else an *integral ecology* (Pope Francis 2015).

The search for indicators beyond GDP is part of the same movement. It calls for a clear connection between a conceptual framework and governance. In her contribution, Géraldine Thiry underlines what is at stake in this matter. On the one hand, the push to transition will not suffice if GDP is simply to be amended with indicators of well-being and sustainability, without leaving behind the former theoretical representation; what is needed is a more radical conversion of accounting frameworks, in accordance with final goals. On the other hand, new indicators of prosperity will only find their legitimacy if they result in bringing about a debate on values and worldviews, in a participatory logic and in consolidation of the collective. Autonomy cannot be exercised without using proper evaluation tools to judge the merits of the decision taken and the progress made.

The setting up of a coherent analytical and reflexive framework is also necessary to enrich the dialogue between the different levels of governance, from the local to the global. Such a framework would be useful in all situations, regardless of whether the paths to transition amplify the autonomy of decisions, require the state to lead the charge in responding to ecological and social emergencies, or create a subtle combination of these two possibilities. As Olivier De Schutter underlines, while it is good to decentralize the search for solutions, it is just as important to construct apparatuses that would both allow local initiatives to foster collective action and ensure the support of higher levels of power. Adequately connecting the different levels of a polycentric governance could eventually bring about the indispensable systemic change we seek.

To sum up

The argument developed throughout this book can be summed up in ten propositions that are explored in greater depth in the different chapters.

1 The pursuit of economic growth is an *outdated societal project* for both ecological and social reasons.
2 Renouncing the objective of growth is clearly not easy, as it has served to oil the socio-economic wheels for at least seven decades. It raises several major questions with respect to employment, public finance, economic dynamism and social stability, among others. Elaborating a societal project – within which it is essential to position any economic project – beyond economic growth requires *going back to the roots of our societal goals*, much as some of those economists called "classical" did before us.
3 To this respect, three core principles may serve as guiding posts: the *respect of ecological limits*, the *equity in distribution* (of wealth and, more broadly, of the right to a good life) and the *promotion of autonomy* (involving all in the building of socio-political norms). These principles must always be connected to each other and implemented jointly. In this matter, there is no possible *trade-off*.
4 The magnitude of the questions raised and the necessary transformation of a world marked by globalization, complexity and uncertainty, simultaneously calls for *an innovative global vision* and for *local transition experimentations*. Both already exist. They should be supported and their dialogue facilitated instead of allowing forces of resistance to stifle their development.
5 Numerous works help us to *rethink categories that our generation of economists takes for granted*: the meaning of work and the place it takes in our lives; the very definition of productivity (in relation to our goals); the human content of our exchanges; our relationship to consumption, nature and all living creatures. Far from utopian, such studies echo the inner concerns of citizens expressed in various fashions from burn-out or else depression to transition movements. They help us to realize how much the productivity-driven cage of consumerism is alienating, and how we might unlock it.
6 Complementary to global visions, *a great many transition initiatives* – sometimes driven by these same visions and sometimes developed in a purely pragmatic manner – are at play in our countries and throughout the world. They reinforce the concreteness and the dynamic of the ecological and social transition by putting the aforementioned three principles (see point 3 above) into practice to varying extents.
7 Most of these initiatives, as well as the social economy, contribute to a *decommodification of day-to-day activities* by *purposefully and systematically instilling meaning in them*: cooperation, co-production, sharing, etc. Far from being a nostalgic return to "good old times", these initiatives tap into the great and still unrealized potential of the Internet and other recent technologies.

8   The answer to the challenges currently facing humanity is germinating. Speeding up this process would require that *existing visions and initiatives be put in coherence* both at the levels of theoretical frameworks and of governance.

9   The theoretical frameworks currently dominant in economics struggle to fully apprehend the radical uncertainty that characterizes today's society and are of little use for thinking out and guiding the transition in its triple dimension (i.e. ecological, social and autonomous). They fail to account for this *in-between* where transition precisely occurs. To bring about the revolution in theory that is required to analyse unprecedented challenges, it seems indispensable to adopt a reflexive posture and collaborate with other disciplines, particularly the life sciences. Among the different schools in economics, evolutionary economics and social-ecological economics together with studies dealing with the Commons, open promising avenues for research, which should be expanded and consolidated.

10   Building a coherent theoretical framework attuned to the challenges of our century would greatly facilitate the governance of a post-growth society. It would serve to set priorities and to articulate the connection between all decision levels (i.e. from local to supranational) so as to induce a systemic shift. Although the role of the state remains crucial – a state-led response to ecological and social crises could still be necessary – it is rather a polycentric governance, anchored in territories and confident in citizens' capacity of autonomy, that will most likely serve to guide the transition.

Notes

1   This book originates from the joint direction of a committee on post-growth for the 21st Congress of French-speaking Belgian economists, "Growth: realities and perspectives".

2   Although a communality of views has emerged from our discussions, the scientific responsibility regarding the specific content of this chapter remains entirely ours. We are well aware that other disciplines (such as anthropology, life sciences, etc.) are essential for thinking about post-growth. We also acknowledge that the task undertaken in this book is necessarily incomplete.

3   The term "post-growth" is purposefully referred to in this book since we seek to identify and build on what is already working, rather than focusing on what is not. However, in no way does this mean that we discard all the very insightful works gathered under the term "degrowth" (Latouche 2009; D'Alisa *et al.* 2014). The authors are also keen on underlining that there are multiple paths towards a post-growth society.

4   By economic growth, we refer to the inflation-adjusted increase of Gross Domestic Product (GDP).

5   See Chapter 4 and Table 4.1 in OECD (2014) for economic forecasts up until 2060. More recent data – albeit limited to 2022 – can also be found in IMF (2017: Table A1, p. 198).

6   Literal translation of the French title of Illich's 1971 book (*Libérer l'avenir*) published in English under the title "Celebration of Awareness".

7   Coutrot *et al.* (2011) have rightfully pointed to the multiple nature of transition paths.

8   Heteronomy here refers to one's incapacity to create his or her own laws and to govern accordingly.

9 For Gorz (1993), the expertocracy results from the state having delegated to experts both the role of judging the content of general interest as well as of the means of sub-jecting individuals to it.
10 www.lesconvivialistes.org/abridged-version-of-the-convivialist-manifesto.

References

Arnsperger, C. (2005). *Critique de l'existence capitaliste: Pour une éthique existentielle de l'économie*. Paris: Cerf.
Arnsperger, C. (2015). Collective Action and the Redefinition of Prosperity: On the Democratic Governance of the Transition. In I. Cassiers (ed.), *Redefining Prosperity*. London: Routledge, pp. 143–161.
Boyer, R. and Saillard, Y. (2002). *Regulation Theory: The State of the Art*. London: Routledge.
Braudel, F. (1977). *Afterthoughts on Material Civilization and Capitalism*. Baltimore: Johns Hopkins University Press.
Cassiers, I. (ed.) (2015). *Redefining Prosperity*. London: Routledge.
Cassiers, I. and Delain, C. (2006). La croissance ne fait pas le bonheur: les économistes le savent-ils? *Regards Économiques*, 38: 1–14.
Castoriadis, C. (1998). *The Imaginary Institution of Society*. Cambridge, MA: MIT Press.
Chabot, P. (2015). *L'Âge des transitions*. Paris: PUF.
Costanza, R., Alperovitz, G., Daly, H.E., Farley, J., Franco, C., Jackson, T., Kubiszewski, I., Schor, J. and Victor, P. (2012). *Building a Sustainable and Desirable Economy-in-Society-in-Nature*. New York: United Nations Division for Sustainable Development.
Coutrot, T., Flacher, D. and Méda, D. (eds) (2011). *Pour en finir avec ce vieux monde: Les chemins de la transition*. Paris: Utopia.
D'Alisa, G., Demaria, F. and Kallis, G. (2014). *Degrowth: A Vocabulary for a New Era*. London: Routledge.
Dedeurwaerdere, T. (2014). *Sustainability Science for Strong Sustainability*. Cheltenham, UK and Northampton, MA: Edward Elgar.
Demailly, D., Chancel, L., Waisman, H. and Guivarch, C. (2013). A Post-Growth Society for the 21st Century: Does Prosperity Have to Wait for the Return of Economic Growth? *Studies* no. 08/13. Paris: IDDRI.
Easterlin, R.E. (1974). Does Economic Growth Improve the Human Lot? Some Empirical Evidence. In P.A. David and M.W. Reder (eds), *Nations and Households in Economic Growth: Essays in Honor of Moses Abramovitz*. New York: Academic Press, pp. 89–125.
Gadrey, J. (2014). *Brèves questions/réponses sur la croissance et ses alternatives*. Available online at: http://alternatives-economiques.fr/blogs/ gadrey/files/postcroissance.pdf.
Gerber, V. (2013). *Murray Brookchin et l'écologie sociale*. Montréal: Écosociété.
Gorz, A. (1980). *Ecology as Politics*. Montréal: Black Roses Books.
Gorz, A. (1993). Political Ecology: Expertocracy versus Self-Limitation. *New Left Review*, I/202. Available online at: https://newleftreview.org/I/202/andre-gorz-political-ecology-expertocracy-versus-self-limitation.
Hopkins, R. (2008). *The Transition Handbook: From Oil Dependency to Local Resilience*. Vermont: Chelsea Green Publishing.
Illich, I. (1971). *Celebration of Awareness*. London: Marion Boyars Publishers Ltd.
IMF (2017). *World Economic Outlook: Gaining Momentum?* Washington, DC: IMF. Available online at: www.imf.org/en/Publications/WEO/Issues/2017/04/04/world-economic-outlook-april-2017.

Jackson, T. (2009). *Prosperity Without Growth: Economics for a Finite Planet*. London: Earthscan.

Jackson, T. (2017). *Prosperity Without Growth: Foundations for the Economy of Tomorrow*. London: Routledge.

Latouche, S. (2009). *Farewell to Growth*. Cambridge: Polity Press.

Laurent, E. (2017). *Notre bonne fortune. Repenser la prospérité*. Paris: PUF.

Lietaer, B., Ulanowicz, R.E., Goerner, S. and Mac Laren, N. (2010). Is Our Monetary Structure a Systemic Cause for Financial Instability? Evidence and Remedies from Nature. *Journal of Futures Studies*, 14(3): 89–108.

Maddison, A. (2001). *The World Economy: A Millennial Perspective*. Paris: OCDE.

Maréchal, K. (2012). *The Economics of Climate Change and the Change of Climate in Economics*. London and New York: Routledge.

Meadows, D., Randers, J. and Behrens, W. (1972). *Limits to Growth*. New York: New American Library.

Méda, D. (2008). *Au-delà du PIB. Pour une autre mesure de la richesse*. Paris: Champs-Actuel.

Méda, D. (2013). *La Mystique de la croissance. Comment s'en libérer*. Paris: Flammarion.

Mill, J.S. (1848). *Principles of Political Economy with Some of Their Applications to Social Philosophy*. London: Longmans, Green and Co. Available online at: www. econlib.org/library/Mill/mlP.html.

NDPSCS (New Development Paradigm Steering Committee and Secretariat) (2013). *Happiness: Towards a New Development Paradigm, Report of the Kingdom of Bhutan*. Available online at: www.newdevelopmentparadigm.bt/2013/12/13/new-development-pardigm-report/.

NEF (New Economic Foundation) (2015). *Principles for a New Economy*. Working paper, August.

OECD (2011). *Divided We Stand: Why Inequality Keeps Rising*. Paris: OECD.

OECD (2014). *OECD Economic Outlook*. Vol. 2014/1. Paris: OECD. Available online at: www.oecd-ilibrary.org/economics/oecd-economic-outlook-volume-2014-issue-1_eco_outlook-v2014-1-en.

Piketty, T. (2014). *Capital in the Twenty-First Century*. Cambridge, MA: Harvard University Press.

Pope Francis (2015). *Encyclical Letter Laudato Si' of the Holy Father Francis on Care for Our Common Home*. Vatican City: Libreria Editrice Vaticana. Available online at: http:// w2.vatican.va/content/francesco/en/encyclicals/documents/papa-francesco_20150524_enciclica-laudato-si.html.

Rasteau, M. (2015). *L'économie collaborative comme concrétisation de la revendication d'autonomie de l'écologie politique*. End-of-studies dissertation. Université Libre de Bruxelles.

Steffen, W., Richardson, K., Rockström, J., Cornell, S., Fetzer, I., Bennett, E., Biggs, R., Carpenter, S., De Vries, W., De Wit, C., Folke, C., Gerten, D., Heinke, J., Mace, G., Persson, L., Ramanathan, V., Reyers, B. and Sörlin, S. (2015). Planetary Boundaries: Guiding Human Development on a Changing Planet. *Science*, 347(6223): 736–746.

Veblen, T. (1898). Why Is Economics Not an Evolutionary Science? *The Quarterly Journal of Economics*, 12(4): 373–397.

Wilkinson, R. and Pickett, K. (2009). *The Spirit Level: Why More Equal Societies Almost Always Do Better*. London: Allen Lane.

2 Work and employment in a post-growth era

Dominique Méda

Consciousness of the risk that climate change poses to humanity has grown increasingly intense. We now know that our mode of development may result in – and has already caused – profound modifications in the way the biosphere functions and that, as Hans Jonas explained years ago in *The Imperative of Responsibility: In Search of an Ethics for the Technological Age* (1990), what is threatened is less the Earth's survival than the possibility of leading an authentically human life. Use of the (controversial) term "Anthropocene" to refer to this era calls attention to the responsibility of human activity in this process.

Yet we are also, at the same time, becoming aware of the extraordinarily ambivalent character of growth. It has, of course, brought immense benefits, whose value no one can seriously question. But growth has also brought many problems, which until recently we overlooked – save for a brief interlude in the 1970s, when the *damage* that growth has done to our natural heritage, social relations and work was first denounced, as can be seen in the Meadows report (Meadows *et al.* 1972), Bertrand de Jouvenel's reflections (1968) and the well-known work of Ivan Illich and Jacques Ellul. Two oil crises and the resulting economic slump justified this criticism. But it is now becoming clear that greenhouse gas (GHG) emissions and economic growth – which Angus Maddison (2002) has precisely charted – have developed according to a similar pattern, with a take-off in the mid-nineteenth century and very significant acceleration around the Second World War. These parallels have led some to speak of "an alternative history of the postwar era" (Pessis *et al.* 2013), a moment in which excess became the norm.

We now have to face up to a major contradiction: at present, we need growth because much of our economic and social system depends on it and our social dynamic is organized around it. Technologically and ideologically, we are a *society based on growth*; our entire episteme and all our categories belong to a paradigm that holds growth to be its primary objective (Méda 2013). Yet we are also ever more conscious that growth has and continues to lead to a series of social and environmental problems that could destroy the very foundation that allows society to reproduce itself. Sequential reasoning – i.e. "let's first restore growth as a way of solving the most urgent problems (economic and social issues), then we can deal with ecological questions" (which until now seemed to have been validated by the famous Kuznets curves, according to which higher growth rates mean greater attention to environmental issues) – no longer seems appropriate.

Yet is it still possible to maintain the goals of growth while changing its contents? Can we continue to benefit from growth while minimising the greenhouse gas emissions it produces, the waste and pollution it creates, and the extractions and scarce resources it depends on? This hope for "green" or "clean growth", which is rooted in a faith in the virtues of technological progress, runs up against the difficulties associated with imagining a complete decoupling of GDP and GHG (Jackson 2017 [2009]; Caminel *et al.* 2014) and the existence of scarce resource peaks (Bihouix 2014; Bardi 2015). It would require a wave of technological progress unlike anything seen in the past twenty years.

In 2010, Michel Husson, in a paper entitled "Growth without CO_2", which analyses the consequences of two scenarios for reducing GHG, arrived at the following conclusion:

> Achieving the IPCC's goals is incompatible at various levels with the pursuit of growth. In the most demanding emission reduction scenario (–85%), and without accelerating the trend towards less carbon intensive GDP, the world's GDP would have to decline by 3.3% per year, or 77% between 2007 and 2050! The scenario with a 50% reduction goal and an accelerated decline of carbon emissions is compatible with global GDP growth of 0.9%, but this is significantly lower than trends observed in recent years.
>
> (Husson 2010: 4, our translation)

Our thinking expands upon the perspectives these various studies have opened. Taking them seriously means that, in our norms and our actions, we can no longer give priority to the quest for growth (which is expressed by the prevailing use, in international debates and comparisons, of the indicator "GDP per inhabitant" to evaluate performance), but rather to obey the strict environmental norms to which production must henceforth be subjected. This means nothing less than reincorporating into the production process ethical and political considerations relating to common well-being and breaking with a number of premises, derived notably from neoclassical economics, upon which collective action has, for over two centuries, relied. This change of perspective makes it necessary to adopt a different set of indicators to guide individual and collective action (Méda 1999, 2013; Gadrey and Jany-Catrice 2016; Cassiers 2015; Laurent and Le Cacheux 2015) that gives absolute priority to Jonas' imperative: "act in such a way that the effects of your action be compatible with the permanence of authentically human life on Earth".

Adopting other indicators that re-embed production within constraints – particularly environmental ones – makes it possible to replace the dictatorship of growth with the satisfaction of social needs while respecting our natural heritage and social cohesion. It is in this way that we can begin speaking of a post-growth society: a society that places at the heart of its concerns and selects as the criteria for guiding public action and evaluating economic performance not the quest for growth, but other goals, and which thus relativizes the centrality of growth rates to its objectives. Such a transformation of perspective implies that society undertakes an ecological conversion that would entail considerable upheaval in the realms of employment and work.

What are the consequences of a transition towards a post-growth society? Will it still be possible to create jobs? What changes in work should one expect? What social model is likely to arise as this society expands? It is to these questions that we now turn.

Employment in the post-growth era

Fear about employment is one of the themes mentioned most frequently in speeches by political and administrative officials – and economic arguments more generally – that call for high growth rates. To take the case of France,[1] a growth rate of 1.5 per cent per year is apparently needed to begin reducing unemployment. This figure takes into account both demography (800,000 young people enter the job market each year, while 650,000 seniors leave it) and productivity gains, which contribute to reducing the number of jobs required to produce a given good. Growth would thus seem to be indispensable to job creation. Lack of growth, very low growth rates, and an era of post-growth would result systematically in higher unemployment – making each of these situations highly undesirable.

Reduced working time

In a very clear article ("Sixty Years of Employment"), Husson introduces an important distinction between the short term and the long term: "Growth creates jobs. In the short term, this is obvious, and the 2008–2009 recession's impact on employment illustrates this point very brutally" (2009: 22, our translation). And yet, he continues, it is possible, if one steps back, "to assert that growth does not create jobs over the long term" (2009: 26). He adds:

> This seemingly iconoclastic proposition follows from the close connection between GDP growth and growth in hourly productivity [...] The growth in hourly productivity follows a trajectory that closely resembles GDP's. Employment, however, depends on the development of these two figures in relation to one another: to know the jobs content of GDP growth, one must subtract increases in hourly productivity.
>
> (Husson 2009: 26, our translation)

That is, when the growth rate of hourly productivity is greater than that of GDP, unemployment goes up; in the opposite case, jobs are created, presuming that the number of working hours remains constant. The latter is thus a crucial variable:

when labour's productivity increases at the same rate as production, net job creation depends primarily on reduced working time. Husson calls attention to the effects of this variable on the rise of the French unemployment rate between 1974 and 1984 (when reduced working time was too low to absorb productivity gains) and the period of robust job creation between 1997 and 2002 (which he attributes in part to reduced working time, which was introduced in 1998). It is thus possible to create jobs without growth, provided that working time is reduced.

Official assessments have estimated that the creation of between 350,000 and 400,000 jobs can be imputed directly to the laws of reduction of the working time in France (INSEE 2005). It has shown, moreover, that the reduction of working time was an employment measure that proved particularly inexpensive (Heyer 2012), facilitated the harmonization of professional and family life, and brought some equilibrium in the distribution of work between men and women, notably as relates to family tasks (Méda and Orain 2002; Méda *et al.* 2004). Others see the decrease in working time as a way of increasing the amount of time devoted to self-production, political and civic activities, charitable work, family life and noncommercial endeavours. In this way, the reduction of working time proves beneficial in many respects, most notably by reducing the time devoted to production and consumption – assuming, that is, that time "freed up" in this way is devoted to activities other than the kind of production and consumption that increases our carbon footprint (Larrouturou and Méda 2016).

In France, there is still heated debate over the impact of the "thirty-five hours" work-week law (see Romagnan 2014) and on whether now is the time to launch a new round of reduction of working time. Particular emphasis is given to the risks arising from the intensification of work (which seems, however, to be undermined by "Work Conditions" investigations, which show that the period between 1998 and 2005 was an interlude in the continuous decline of working conditions since the 1980s) and, in particular, the risks of heavier labour costs for companies if the reduction of working time occurs without a proportional reduction of salaries. The key question is that of financing the portion of this initiative not covered by the reallocation of public expenditures previously devoted to unemployment – a point to which we will return in the third part of this chapter.

Job reallocation during the ecological conversion

Though it is a necessary complement to productivity gains, particularly for redistributing the current volume of labour across the entire working population, the reduction of working time is not, however, the only policy capable of creating jobs in the absence of growth. It can be of great use to the ecological conversion, which will lead to the development of specific forms of production in particular sectors (through the reduction, in turn, of other forms of production in other sectors), the decisive criterion being the quantity of greenhouse gases generated. But the ecological conversion itself will result in job reallocation, the precise distribution of which has been the subject of studies that are still too rare and varied in their results.

Most of the projections for France since 2007 (ADEME 2013; Quirion 2013) foresee a positive net job balance in 2020, 2030 and 2060, consistent with European and international studies (UNEP 2008), which emphasize that the economic activities that must be developed (such as building insulation, renewable energy and public transportation) have a much higher job content than those whose volume must be decreased. It is worth noting that the most optimistic research was published before European countries had been fully hit by the economic and financial crisis and the price of oil fell.

Moreover, the summary of the UNEP-ILO report aimed at decision-makers underscores the fact that even if the balance is positive,

> Not everybody will gain from such a change, however. The typically positive job balance from greening an economy is the result of major shifts often within sectors. While some groups and regions are gaining significantly, others incur substantial losses. These losses raise questions of equity, which if not addressed, can make green economy policies difficult to sustain.
>
> (UNEP 2008: 16)

Whether it be countries, sectors or categories of workers, ecological conversion is thus an extremely delicate operation requiring powerful security mechanisms to ensure that the process, which is comparable to a restructuring, does not exclude from the labour market a significant share of the workforce employed in sectors emitting the most GHG. The notion of a "fair transition", favoured by the labour movement, defends the idea that the ecological conversion must occur in a civilized manner: it must be organized, gains and losses must be mutualized, and a genuine sense of solidarity must arise from every concerned member of society, so that the costs of transition are shared by all.

A new paradigm and millions of sustainable jobs

Gadrey's work is among the most suggestive and innovative studies of our society's capacity to create employment without growth. In *Adieu à la croissance* (Gadrey 2010), as well as in his blog, Gadrey maintains that our society can create millions of sustainable jobs if we rebuild a productive system that minimizes recourse to fossil fuels and places production at the service of social needs.

Building a productive system that ensures the same level of comfort, only without fossil fuels or nuclear energy, implies a complete rebuilding of our energy infrastructure, as Ugo Bardi (2015) explains in a report to the Club of Rome. It would primarily use renewable energies (solar, wind, water and biomass power) and would orchestrate the gradual banning of other energy sources (including the renunciation of use of underground reserves). This would be a major source of jobs. To this must be added the transformation of the entire (non-energy) production system: transportation, construction, industry and services, which simultaneously implies the thermal renovation of buildings, the construction of new kinds of buildings for production and housing purposes, and the implementation of new production processes, all of which are characterized by weak GHG emissions. Agriculture is an important aspect of this transformation, to the extent that it contributes to GHG and pollution of various kinds (excess water usage, fertilization, excess land use, pesticides and so on). Gadrey writes:

> By drawing on good quality scenarios, including the NégaWatt scenario and various studies of agricultural conversion, I estimate that an ecological transition equal to the task should be able to create more than a million new jobs over fifteen to twenty years (all things being equal, as relates to work-time). This would involve an energy and climate transition, including major developments in renewable energies; transitions in agriculture and forestry, in transportation, mobility, and construction; the thermal renovation of housing and old buildings; recycling; recuperation; a circular economy; the improvement of urban air quality, the upkeep of nature in urban and rural environments.
>
> (Gadrey 2014)

It is important in this context not to overlook the ever-rising sums of money we devote to repairing the damage brought about by growth, which Tobin and Nordhaus describe as "regrettable" (Gadrey 2014). A report by the French Senate has recently priced the cost of air pollution alone at a hundred billion euro (Sénat 2015). Addressing previously underestimated social needs could be another source of jobs: foster care for young children, care for the elderly, comprehensive education, culture and wellness services represent, according to Gadrey, employment opportunities for a million people over the next twenty years. Finally, the cessation of reckless automatization and the obsessive quest for profits would result in the non-elimination of jobs – a point to which we will return.

The recent study *One Million Climate Jobs: Tackling the Environmental and Economic Crisis* (2014) indicates that it is possible to create more than one million climate jobs, i.e. jobs devoted to the improvement of climate. It involves a twenty-year plan that foresees a drastic reduction of the United Kingdom's GHG emissions, the hiring of a million people in a single year by a national climate service charged with implementing these reductions, and the transfer of individuals whose jobs are threatened to other forms of employment. According to these studies, it will be the government's responsibility to organize the operations that will make it possible to achieve reduction goals as quickly as possible (by taking direct responsibility, at no cost, for building renovations, building sustainable transportation services and rebuilding the energy system).

The post-growth era: an opportunity to end productivism and de-intensify work?

As we have seen, hourly productivity constitutes a crucial variable in the relationship between growth and employment. Productivity gains are considered to be the primary source of growth: increases in both figures are closely tied. This is why the possibility of slower productivity gains provokes such fear – as seen with the shock produced by Gordon's forward-looking work, declaring that due to various "countervailing winds", growth in productivity will decline considerably in years to come (for instance, the average annual growth rate in the United States will not exceed 0.2 per cent) or the efforts devoted to solving the puzzle of the lack of productivity gains arising from the digital revolution – might they not be greater than is commonly believed? (Teulings and Baldwin 2014). Productivity gains are, in societies founded on growth, a kind of lung, from a micro as well as from a macro perspective. Remember Adam Smith's famous description of the pin factory, in which improvements in the organization of labour, notably its division, appears as the cause of compounded productive efficiency and thus of increasing wealth. If there is one firmly anchored economic belief that has never been questioned and that has been constantly refined theoretically, it is that of productivity and its central role in our current paradigm (Fourastié 1979).

Breaking with productivity gains?

The main battles fought since the 1960s have had to do with the distribution of productivity gains, and particularly the evolution of the relative share of salaries within these gains. The Fordist period was the high point of the battle in which workers lost ground.

But what if the real question was not how to redistribute productivity gains, but whether they are necessary? What if genuine progress, at present, no longer depended on higher productivity gains but, as Gadrey claims, on quality and sustainability gains? What if we have arrived at a moment at which the systematic pursuit of productivity gains in all sectors – and particularly services – has become counterproductive? What if an analysis of the productivity gains achieved during the post-war boom revealed that the environment and workers have been overexploited and the time has come to repair these damages? What if productivity gains could be almost entirely correlated to the depletion of non-renewable energy sources and resources, as well as to the transformation of human beings into producing and consuming machines?

At the very moment when the Fordist system was being established, productivity gains were intensifying, French researchers and industrialists were travelling to the United States to import American methods, and Jean Fourastié was writing a beginner's guide (1980 [1952]) to the concept of productivity, Georges Friedmann (1956) and Bertrand de Jouvenel in the texts later assembled in *Arcadie* called attention to the harmful effects of such goals. Friedmann devoted much of his book to explaining the mistake of the author of *The Division of Labor in Society* (for whom the division of labour, as the foundation of social solidarity, was only pathological accidentally): "If Durkheim had lived, he would have been obliged to consider as abnormal most of the forms that labor has assumed in our society."

Jouvenel, for his part, drew attention to two points. On the one hand, he claimed, productivity gains constitute a "progress in the organization of labor but a regression in the planning of existence [...] What man gains in satisfaction as a consumer, he loses as a producer" (1968: 55). On the other hand,

> given the increased power available to us, human existence improved less than men from earlier times to whom this increase had been announced would have believed [...] They would have expected civilization's wealth to be displayed in the beauty of its cities and the language of its citizens [...] that our civilization, incomparably wealthier than its predecessors, would eclipse them with the beauty of its public edifices and add to them the grace of family housing harmoniously wedded to their structures.
>
>   (Jouvenel 1968: 57, our translation)

We have "chosen" to use productivity gains to increase the volume of goods and services produced rather than to improve the quality of life and work. We have also chosen more production at lower prices instead of more free time: according to Boutaud (2016), the productivity gains achieved since this time should have made it possible to achieve the production levels of 1950 with only eight hours of work per week.

The close alliance between the plea economists have, since the eighteenth century, made on productivity's behalf; accounting policies employed by companies; national governments that equate wealth creation with greater volume, while giving insufficient consideration to qualitative improvements in goods and services; and the methods of Taylor's scientific organization of labour, which held that the only criteria of efficiency was lower prices for consumers, regardless of their consequences for the nature of work – all these factors have emphasized the importance of increasing the quantity of goods produced in a given time, and, ultimately, of lowering prices for goods and services, at the expense of every other concern.

Should one posit a line of causality between the exponential development of productivity and work's loss of meaning (which many authors have denounced) and the deterioration of working conditions? Even if not every increase in production implies the intensification of work (new machines can, to the contrary, make work more comfortable), the process has historically gone hand in hand with further division of labour, which, for André Gorz (1988), is the deeper cause of work's heteronomous character. As the economy, bureaucracy, the state and science developed, he maintains, they demand an increasing subdivision of their competencies and tasks, and increasingly differentiated organizations of increasingly specialized functions. Workers' behaviour became functional – that is, rationally adapted to goals – in ways that became completely independent of the agent's intent to pursue the goal. "I call the heteronomous sphere", Gorz writes, "the totality of specialized activities that individuals must carry out as functions that are coordinated externally by a pre-established organization" (1988: 49).

In light of work's unquestionable heteronomy, which has been contaminated by economic and technical rationality, Gorz concludes that one must keep striving for increasingly intense productivity gains and apply them to reducing working time in a way that will increase the sphere of free time and autonomy, of enjoyable activities and work for oneself. Gadrey, to the contrary, proposes that we end our obsessive quest for productivity gains (as currently measured), as measurement standards adopted in the 1950s are no longer adapted to a society heading increasingly towards a service economy (most production arises from services in which the identification of increasing quantities is extremely tricky, if not impossible), nor to the need to profoundly alter production's content (to make it ecologically "cleaner"). Striving for qualitative improvements and sustainability rather than productivity gains would replace the obsession with greater volumes with a concern for quality, increase the amount of labour required, make work less intensive and meaningful once again, and ensure that production occurs while tending to natural "resources" and labour.

Caring for our natural heritage and labour

Gadrey adopts the perspective of a new relationship between human beings and nature that acknowledges the critique of modernity and the conquering and exploitative ends to which, in modern times, humans have subjected nature. As has been shown by authors as different as Adorno and Horkheimer, Heidegger, and more recently, Pope Francis in the *Encyclical Laudato Si' on Care for Our Common Home* (2015), modernity legitimated a type of knowledge and human action that, following Bacon's plan, seeks to extract from nature its secrets and its products, controlling and inspecting them, shaping them for human use rather than incorporating human activity into an existing reality that must be preserved and cared for. The paradigm of manipulation and domination, in which humans see nature as something reserved entirely for their own use, must give way to a model in which humans make use of nature while respecting rules that ensure its reproduction and arranging processes that are less hostile towards the natural world, human work and social cohesion.

The "taking care" paradigm consists in economising human labour and natural resources and ensuring that carbon and ecological footprints and the pollution produced by extraction and waste are as light as possible. It also respects what economics sees as nothing more than a "factor of production", making it a radically different paradigm than that of productive efficiency (or at least one in which efficiency takes on a completely different meaning). Progress can no longer consist exclusively in increasing volume, quantities and yields: raising the latter to the highest possible level – at the risk of devoting enormous sums to compensating resulting damage – can no longer be our goal. The idea, rather, is to embed the act of production itself in rules and ethical norms. These new social and environmental norms constitute a new normative and accounting frame-work: new principles must replace the principles of productivity and profitability implemented in the 1950s, in which the decisive criteria would no longer be greater corporate or national production volumes, but higher quality goods and services, GHG emission reduction as a standard for measuring quality, and, more generally, minimising the potential deterioration of the environment and human labour due to production.

If absolute priority must now be given to producing goods and services with lighter ecological and carbon footprints and making the quality of goods and ser-vices the crucial criterion, then the view that encourages the production of goods in the largest possible qualities and at the greatest possible speed has become obsolete. We need new accounting principles that highlight quality gains in a way that can guide and evaluate the behaviour of productive organizations and nations, whose purpose will be to build a production system capable of satisfy-ing basic needs insofar as they *take care* of the environment and human labour.

New labour organizations in the service of quality

How will organizations be able to implement new understandings of quality – drawing on new national and corporate accounting principles? Which organiza-tions are most likely to produce goods and services seeking to satisfy primary needs – presuming that they respect the environment – rather than greater yield or profitability? Under what conditions can decent productive organizations emerge?

By using the European inquiry on labour conditions, Gallie and Zhou (2013) show that certain labour organizations are more favourable than others to work quality and that their frequency is correlated to national unionization rates. One could go further still and call attention to the elective affinities between (micro) forms of labour organization and (macro) forms of develop-ment. Weber defended his view that capitalism is about the permanent quest for profit maximization, and thus with a particular kind of company: "capit-alism is identical with the pursuit of profit, and forever *renewed* profit, by means of continuous, rational, capitalistic enterprise" (1992 [1905]: 17). A configuration of this kind seems perfectly suited to the national goal of per-manently increasing growth rates:

> The important fact is always that a calculation of capital in terms of money is made, whether by modern book-keeping methods or in any other way, however primitive and crude. Everything is done in terms of balances: at the beginning of the enterprise an initial balance, before every individual deci-sion a calculation to ascertain its probable profitableness, and at the end a final balance to ascertain how much profit has been made.
>
> (Weber 1992 [1905]: 18)

Would companies pursuing an other goal than maximising profits not be more appropriate to the development of post-growth society? And if so, presuming that organizations which are not governed by the permanent quest for profit are better able to devote themselves to satisfying social needs and improving the quality and sustainability of goods and services, should we not revise the definition of the company that has prevailed since Milton Friedman and encourage the development of a company of a different kind? The legal scholar Jean-Philippe Robé (2011) has shown that the definition of the company proposed by Milton Friedman and agency theory, which both defend the idea that a company's vocation is exclusively to make profit and that corporate leaders who are most determined to increase profits should be rewarded accordingly, does not allow companies to contribute systematically to the collective interest. Much scholarship by economists, legal scholars, sociologists, management theorists and philosophers has shown, in recent years, that companies should be allowed to legitimately pursue other goals than that of profit and that their current form, which seeks primarily to increase their value for shareholders, should give way to other forms of organization making it possible coordinate new accounting principles and new production goals. Proposals to create a new form of corporate law would make it possible to recognize the singular nature of the company as a project of collective creation that is distinct from traditional forms of commercial exchange.

What social model, institutions and actors will best serve a post-growth economy?

Abandoning a process in which rising GDP is guaranteed, and thus, at least theoretically, more and more jobs, income and taxes (both income and payroll) could obviously cause a decline in the financial resources devoted to supporting our social model – and particularly social protection. Can the post-growth society, in which GDP growth is no longer the main goal, be reconciled with a social model ensuring a high level of protection and solidarity? More generally, how are we to organize the transition towards a post-growth society? By drawing on what forces, actors and arguments? By effectuating what changes in the development model that Western societies have pursued since the Industrial Revolution?

What rules will serve a post-growth society?

Building "clean" production – ecologically and socially – requires following strict rules, across a territory that is extensive enough to minimize the risk of dumping, and establishing a system to monitor their application. During the twentieth century, the application of social rules to the territory as a whole (notably relating to working hours and conditions) made it possible to improve labour conditions and take care of workers. If multiple rules, ranging from regulations of classified sties to the REACH programme, have been put into place since the early nineteenth century to avoid production's most general risks, the time has now come to issue new regulations, founded in particular on respecting GHG and other pollution thresholds.

If one of the greatest dangers we must fight is the increase of GHG, then the only solution is to impose very strict emission quotas on every entity that generates them, be they companies or individuals. In the 1950s, power consisted in increasing basic material production. Today, it consists in reducing GHG emissions while continuing to meet people's needs. According to new accounting principles, the primary unit of measurement would thus no longer be currency or added value, but kilograms or tons of GHG. Like carbon quotas except for the fact they would not be tradable, each "unit" would be subject to emission quotas that would be calculated on the basis of a country-by-country allotment. The production process would be required to respect these norms, while preventing labor from being replaced by intensifying it.

A conjunction of social and environmental norms would thus serve as the analytical framework, a guide and a tool for evaluation organizations. Production and consumption would continue to be considered as crucial activities for collective and individual life, but results would be achieved by enhancing quality, not volume, with variations in quality constituting profits and losses. Should one continue to calculate in currency or in physical units (decreasing GHG emissions, increasing nutritional value, caloric value and so on)? Can one replace national and corporate accounting with accounting that is exclusively based on physical units, such as energy? This crucial question will not be answered in this chapter.

Be that as it may, a process of this kind requires a large number of countries committed to respecting these rules: otherwise, there is a real risk of social and environmental dumping, which, incidentally, currently occurs when indecent production is outsourced to countries with less strict regulation. The ideal situation would obviously be one in which global organization would issue norms, organize how they are distributed, control their enforcement and sanction their violation. One imagines a World Environment Organization for GHG emissions quotas and an International Labour Organization – which, of course, already exists, but would be granted greater powers than at present, notably a body for resolving disputes modelled on the WTO's. Another solution would consist in applying these rules to a single region, such as the European Union. In any case, the goals set at the regional level would be adapted to the various territories and units of production and consumption. Legislation similar to that of classified installations, which would include a specialized inspecting body, would be implemented.

Such an organization also presupposes new regulations relating to international trade. From the standpoint we have adopted, which takes the threat of climate change seriously, it is impossible to keep on seeing international trade as a force driving global production and consumption and as a means for countries engaged in competition with one another to acquire market shares. If the goal is no longer to increase national market shares and profits but to satisfy the needs of the citizens of countries united in the struggle against climate change, then we must replace competition with cooperation and adopt a different form of organization.

A number of associations have recently proposed the creation of an alternative trade mandate in the European Union. This would consist of an entirely new procedure for initiating, negotiation and concluding trade agreements, in a way that would grant a decisive role to civil society and parliaments, ensure Europe's self-sufficiency in food products, and lead to a reduction in the importation of raw materials and manufactured goods, an emphasis on human rights over commercial interests, and guarantees of responsible behaviour on the part of multinational corporations.

A planned exit for societies founded on growth

A process of this kind (involving an ethical framework for production, the conversion of polluting sectors to clean sectors, the dematerialization and decarbonization of the economy, measures ensuring the safety of labour transfers, the creation of public policies and institutions ensuring the transition towards practices with lower human costs, and so on) requires a war or crisis economy, similar to that described by Lord Beveridge in his 1944 report, *Full Employment in a Free Society*. Many authors have suggested the scale of the threefold crisis (economic, social and ecological) that we are facing requires implementing policies and means that are radically different from those that occur in normal times, in particularly because it is necessary to organize and coordinate multiple operations at several different levels.

As a liberal, Beveridge believed that to guarantee liberty, the state needed to establish very strict rules, which alone could ensure society's long-term durability. Seeing full employment as a fundamental pillar of a free society, Beveridge specified four conditions that could ensure it: maintaining at all times a sufficient level of spending through massive public expenditures and investments, policies ensuring low prices for essential consumer items, and significant income redistribution (thanks to Social Security and progressive taxation); controlling industry's physical location; organising labour's mobility; maintaining trade relations only with countries that pursue full employment policies, keeping accounts balanced by avoiding deficits and surpluses, and exercising complete control over trade through tariffs, quotas and other means. Far from believing that personal freedom was challenged by the state's willingness to assume the overriding responsibility that befell it in such circumstances, Beveridge saw it, rather, as its necessary precondition.

To commit countries to the path of the ecological transition requires, at present, guidance from the state as firm as during the Second World War and the period of post-war reconstruction, when national accounting and planning were developed in closely intertwined ways and the goal was to rebuild society on a new basis. How could the identification of sectors that must be converted as soon as possible not require on the part of the state the implementation of a genuine planning process? How could it dispense with ambitious forecasting of required jobs and qualifications, forged through a vast process of reflection with labour, management and scholars in every discipline that would identify the sectors and careers of the future? By "intense state intervention", one must understand a more collective definition of priority social needs, resulting from communal deliberation about useful social production. Taking account of ethical considerations through a new definition of progress means nothing other than the need to re-embed production in collective decisions based on specific criteria.

Financing transition and organizing income and access redistribution

How can we finance the recasting of our productive system, at the same time as we continue to pay down our debts and to ensure the operation of our successful social model, while also guaranteeing that Southern countries can access the technology available to us and renouncing agreements that make them subordinate to the well-being of Western societies? Pochet and Degryse (2011) present, along these lines, the trilemma with which present-day society is confronted.

We should mention from the outset that this question can be resolved neither by cobbling together a solution nor by remaining within the framework defined by existing European treaties and economic theory, be it Keynesian or neoclassical. What has become urgent is not simply stimulating consumption to get production going again, nor to lower wages and social protection to increase one country's competitiveness at the expense of another's. The point, as we have said, is to reconceive our accounting policies, the theoretical framework to which they belong, the anthropology, cosmology and, more generally, the broader *episteme* informing the disciplines that we need. Yet the fact remains that we must organize the transition from one social framework to another, pay for the enormous investments that rebuilding our productive system will require, and find a way of agreeing to a genuinely war-like and reconstructive effort.

We must first think in terms of net expenditures or by taking into account defensive or regrettable expenditures, along the lines defined by Tobin and Nordhaus in their work from the early 1970s, which sought to calculate a new indicator that would incorporate the kind of production that generates well-being (domestic labour, volunteer work, leisure activities, and so on) but which is not included in GDP, and that would, at the same time, exclude production that does not result in an ultimate increase in consumption, and thus satisfaction. The reasoning we have adopted is very similar to the latter: the goal is to no longer take the unproductive detour through growth – in other words, to no longer produce toxic goods and services, which subsequently engender compensation costs, but to prevent production that is toxic to health, the environment and working conditions.

Thus we should expect to see decreases in spending tied to compensation (such as the hundred billion euros associated with the costs of air pollution in France, as well as the treatment of obesity or unemployment). Gadrey adopts exactly this kind of reasoning when he points out that long-term unemployment can be fought by directing funds currently devoted to alleviating this problem to creating jobs with high quality contracts. Thus current expenses would be used for other purposes (on the model of activating passive expenditures) and would prevent the appearance of new reasons to spend. In all these cases, the point is to recycle expenditures currently devoted to remedying environmental and social costs. This will not be sufficient. Other means must be envisaged.

What is needed are extremely significant investments that will make it possible to completely rebuild our energy system and to restructure our production and transportation systems. New Climate Economy's latest report calculated the necessary investments to be $93 trillion between 2015 and 2030 for the entire world. Previous available calculations estimated the investments necessary for Europe to be $300 billion per year. Several sources of financing must be tapped simultaneously. The fight against tax fraud (which amounts in Europe, to 2,000 billion euro, according to the European Commission, and, in France, between 60 and 80 billion), the creation of a tax on financial transactions (which could bring in 300 billion euro a year) or transportation, carbon taxation, the end of support for fossil fuels (estimated at $5.3 trillion), and significant income redistribution that leans more heavily on the highest incomes should be part of the solution. Recourse to monetary creation (as proposed by the authors of *One Million Climate Jobs*, 2014) and very long-term borrowing from individuals should also be considered, along with loans at very low interest rates by banks and international financial institutions, as Alain Grandjean and Pascal Canfin have described very precisely in the report *Mobiliser les financements pour le climat. Une feuille de route pour une économie décarbonée* (2015), which they submitted to the French president.

What will be the consequence of the entire ecological conversion process (the reconstruction of energy and production systems, the transfer of the labour force across sectors, changes in behaviour, new international regulations) on incomes? The models that are currently available and which are not built around this hypothesis cannot provide an answer. Juliet Schor (2010) seems to think that in a post-growth society, we will consume "better", and thus less. Nothing is less obvious. If consuming "better" (that is, in a way that is more sustainable, better integrated into the environment, less wasteful, with fewer GHGE) is good for the environment and unquestionably good for households' health, nothing suggests that the current passion for consumption, which is also premised on frequency, would be restrained. Will we need as much income in a society that, as a whole, would consume less and place greater emphasis on quality? The key, to the extent that we must confront a common danger, does indeed involve ensuring society's cohesion, and thus of ensuring significant income redistribution, allowing not only each individual to participate in the collective deliberations required for a commitment to conversion, but also to correct the current situation, which is extraordinarily unequal and in which the richest individuals in developed societies emit far more greenhouse gases than the poorest, contributing in this way to enhancing the North's ecological debt (Chancel and Piketty 2015).

Will we arrive at a considered plan to undertake all of these far-reaching reforms, at a time when the lingering effects of the economic crisis make the desire for growth all the more compelling? If we cannot, then we will significantly increase the risk of wars triggered by the rarefication of scarce resources, and we are likely to face far more explosive shortages than would be the case with a rationally organized reduction of consumption – which would allow us to confront our common destiny.

Three additional conditions seem, in any case, to be needed for our society to commit itself to such a transition: we must adopt appropriate indicators to guide our action; we must promote an alliance between employees and consumers based on the principle of quality (i.e. work quality and product quality); and we must give the greatest possible latitude to democracy in producing organizations and in society as a whole.

Note

1 Although this chapter mainly draws on French cases for illustrations, it obviously aims for a more general perspective.

References

ADEME (2013). *L'évaluation macroéconomique des visions énergétiques de l'ADEME 2030–2050*. Paris: ADEME.

Bardi, U. (2015). *Le grand pillage. Comment nous épuisons les ressources de la planète*. Paris: Institut Veblen/Les Petits Matins.

Beveridge, Lord W. (1944). *Full Employment in a Free Society*. London: The New Statesman and Nation and Reynolds News.

Bihouix, P. (2014). *L'Âge des low tech. Vers une civilisation techniquement soutenable*. Paris: Seuil.

Boutaud, A. (2016). Pourquoi la question de la substitution est centrale (et anti-écologique). In D. Bourg, A. Kaufman and D. Méda (eds), *L'âge de la transition. En route pour la conversion écologique*. Paris: Les Petits Matins, pp. 49–53.

Caminel, T., Frémeaux, P., Giraud, G., Lalucq, A. and Roman, P. (2014). *Produire plus, polluer moins: l'impossible découplage?* Paris: Institut Veblen/Les Petits Matins.

Cassiers, I. (ed.) (2015). *Redefining Prosperity*. London and New York: Routledge.

Chancel, L. and Piketty, T. (2015). Carbon and Inequality: From Kyoto to Paris. *PSE*, November. Available online at: www.parisschoolofeconomics.eu/fr/actualites/etude-inegalites-emissions-CO2-financement-equitable-adaptation-chancel-piketty/.

Fourastié, J. (1979). *Les Trente Glorieuses*. Paris: Hachette.

Fourastié, J. (1980 [1952]). *La Productivité*. Paris: Presses Universitaires de France.

Friedmann, G. (1956). *Le Travail en miettes*. Paris: Gallimard.

Gadrey, J. (2010). *Adieu à la croissance*. Paris: Les Petits Matins.

Gadrey, J. (2014). Comment créer des millions d'emplois durables. Available online at: http://alternatives-economiques.fr/blogs/gadrey/2014/11/21/on-peut-creer-des-millions-d%E2%80%99emplois-utiles-dans-une-perspective-durable-1/.

Gadrey, J. and Jany-Catrice, F. (2016). *Les nouveaux indicateurs de richesse*. Paris: La Découverte.

Gallie, D. and Zhou, Y. (2013). *Work Organisation and Employee Involvement in Europe*. Luxembourg: Eurofund, Publications Office of the European Union.

Giraud, G. (2014). *Illusion financière. Des subprimes à la transition écologique*. Paris: Les Éditions de l'Atelier.

Gorz, A. (1988). *Métamorphoses du travail. Quête du sens*. Paris: Galilée.

Grandjean, A. and Canfin, P. (2015). *Mobiliser les financements pour le climat. Une feuille de route pour une économie décarbonée*. Report to the French president.

Heyer, E. (2012). Le (bon) bilan des trente-cinq heures. *Alternatives économiques*, special issue 92.

Husson, M. (2009). Soixante ans d'emploi. In *La France du travail*. Paris: Les éditions de l'atelier, pp. 21–54.

Husson, M. (2010). Croissance sans CO2? *hussonet*, 24, October. Available online at: http://hussonet.free.fr/crco2.pdf.

INSEE (2005). La réduction du temps de travail. *Économie et Statistique*, 376–377.

Jackson, T. (2017 [2009]). *Prosperity without Growth? The Transition to a Sustainable Economy*. Report of the Sustainable Development Commission (UK). Available online at: www.sd-commission.org.uk/data/files/publications/prosperity_without_growth_report.pdf

Jonas, H. (1990). *The Imperative of Responsibility: In Search of an Ethics for the Technological Age*. Chicago: University of Chicago Press.

Jouvenel, B. de (1968). *Arcadie. Essais sur le mieux-vivre*. Paris: Futuribles, Sedeis.

Larrouturou, P. and Méda, D. (2016). *Einstein avait raison. Il faut réduire le temps de travail*. Paris: Les éditions de l'Atelier.

Laurent, E. and Le Cacheux, J. (2015). *Le nouveau monde économique*. Paris: Odile Jacob.

Maddison, A. (2002). *L'économie mondiale. Une perspective millénaire*. Paris: OCDE.

Meadows, D., Meadows, D., Randers, J. and Behrens, W.W. (1972). *The Limits to Growth*. New York: Universe Books.

Méda, D. (1999). *Qu'est-ce que la richesse?* Paris: Aubier.

Méda, D. (2013). *La Mystique de la croissance. Comment s'en libérer*. Paris: Flammarion.

Méda, D. and Orain, R. (2002). Travail et hors travail: la construction du jugement des salariés sur les trente-cinq heures. *Travail et employ*, 90: 23–38.

Méda, D., Cette, G. and Dromel, N. (2004). Les pères: entre travail et famille. Les enseignements de quelques enquêtes. *Recherches et prévisions*, 76: 7–21.

One Million Climate Jobs: Tackling the Environmental and Economic Crisis (2014). London: Campaign against Climate Change (3rd edn). Available online at: www.campaigncc.org/sites/data/files/Docs/one_million_climate_jobs_2014.pdf.

Pessis, C., Topçu, S. and Bonneuil, C. (2013). *Une autre histoire des "Trente Glorieuses". Modernisation, contestations et pollutions dans la France d'après-guerre*. Paris: La Découverte.

Pochet, P. and Degryse, C. (2011). Sortie de crise: trois options pour l'Europe. In T. Coutrot, D. Flacher and D. Méda (eds), *Pour en finir avec ce vieux monde. Les chemins de la transition*. Paris: Utopia, pp. 93–106.

Pope Francis (2015). *Encyclical Letter Laudato Si' on Care for Our Common Home*. Available online at: http://w2.vatican.va/content/francesco/en/encyclicals/documents/papa-francesco_20150524_enciclica-laudato-si.html.

Quirion, P. (2013). L'effet net sur l'emploi de la transition énergétique en France: Une analyse "input-output" du scénario négaWatt. *CIRED Working Paper Series*, no. 46–2013.

Robé, J.-P. (2011). The Legal Structure of the Firm. *Accounting, Economics, and Law*, 1(1): Article 5

Romagnan, B. (2014). *Rapport fait au nom de la Commission d'enquête sur l'impact sociétal, social, économique et financier de la réduction progressive du temps de travail*, no. 2436. Paris: National Assembly.

Schor, J. (2010). *Plenitude: The New Economics of True Wealth*. New York: Penguin Press.

Sénat (2015). *Rapport de la Commission d'enquête sur le coût économique et financier de la pollution de l'air*, no. 610, 8 July. Paris: Sénat.

Teulings, C. and Baldwin, R. (eds) (2014). *Secular Stagnation: Facts, Causes, and Cures*. London: CEPR Editions. Available online at: http://voxeu.org/ system/files/epublication/ Vox_secular_stagnation.pdf.

UNEP (2008). *Green Jobs: Towards Decent Work in a Sustainable, Low-Carbon World*. Nairobi: UNEP. Available online at: www.ilo.org/wcmsp5/groups/public/@ed_emp/@ emp_ent/documents/publication/wcms_158733.pdf.

Weber, M. (1992 [1905]). *The Protestant Ethic and the Spirit of Capitalism*, trans. Talcott Parsons. New York and London: Routledge.

3 The new paths of decommodification

Bernard Perret

The end of growth as exhaustion of the commodification process

Until recently, only a few academics ventured to evoke the end of growth. Willy-nilly, this perspective is now taken into account by renowned economists. To explain this unforeseen breakdown, mainstream economists usually invoke a set of causes such as the downturn of innovation, the ageing of the population, the move towards a service economy or the growth of energy prices. Obviously, these factors are involved, but their mere addition don't allow to understand the systemic character and the historical reach of the phenomenon. As I show at length in my recent book (Perret 2015),[1] the only explanation matching available evidence is the exhaustion of the "core of the reactor" of capitalist economy, namely the mechanism of transformation of needs into commodities and financial profits. For a set of related reasons, this mechanism operates with decreasing efficacy. In summary, the goods that tend to gain more importance in people's life – the quality of the environment, security, information, medical and social care, etc. – are not genuine commodities, the word "commodity" meaning here appropriable, substitutable and monetarizable goods (in French *marchandise*). Hence, their production hardly takes place within the self-sustained capitalist accumulation process. The case of care services illustrates in a paradigmatic way the fact that a useful good may be unfit for feeding the growth dynamics. In a less obvious way, the same is true of information, and that explains the paradoxical deflationary impact of new technologies – the fact that they result in prices decrease and an extension of gratuity, more often than in the creation of new monetarizable goods.

The social circulation of "non-commodities": a key question for a post-growth social model

There is a wide agreement about the post-materialist values – conviviality, solidarity, personal flourishing and the reconciliation with Nature – that should be promoted in a post-growth society. The movement of "New Wealth Indicators" reflects a widespread frustration towards economic indicators and constitutes a commendable effort to transform post-materialist goals into concrete and measurable policy objectives. But identifying and measuring a new concept of wealth is not enough: one must say how these "non-commodities" will be produced, evaluated and redistributed through new social activities and new institutional devices. Dominique Méda's contribution to this book addresses this question in terms of overall reconfiguration of jobs, activities and incomes. In a complementary manner, the present chapter aims to extend this analysis to the micro-economic and micro-social level. The issue is to show how non-monetarizable goods and utilities are already taken into account by economic agents within existing production and exchange practices. More specifically, I want to show that the question of the social valuation of non-commodities is already addressed through a great diversity of social activities and emerging economic and business practices: solidarity economy, collaborative economy (from Wikipedia to fab-labs), free contributions and peer-to-peer deals on the Internet, functionality economy (the use of material devices as mediums for producing services, as for public car-sharing services), circular economy (recycling, reuse ...). I don't want to say that all these practices are ecologically and socially virtuous: my point is that the levers of efficacy they implement are based upon the social valuation of non-commodities. In this way, they prefigure a process of decommodification of social exchange, which could result in a growth of social welfare without growth of monetary flows.

The word decommodification is used here in a wider sense than in most of economic literature.[2] In the present chapter, decommodification means primarily de-monetarization; it points toward the development of gratuity and non-monetary exchanges, notably through the Internet, self-production and mutualization of goods. By extension, decommodification includes also the intentional production of positive social and environmental externalities. In all cases, it implies a socialized and non-monetary evaluation, economic agents being led to evaluate the goods in a substantial and contextualized way – that is according to their physical scarcity, their usage value and/or their social utility in a given context, and not only through their market price. From the point of view of productive organization, decommodification results in a growth of cooperation, co-production and a more intensive mobilization of the social context (social networks creative of mutual trust). This definition of decommodification covers notably the socio-economic drivers of transition practices analysed from an organizational and institutional point of view in the contribution of Thomas Bauwens and Sybille Mertens (mobilization of social capital in the management of collective goods, hybridization of resources). But it goes further because it points also to the transformations at work in standard economic activities.

The object of this contribution is not to weigh up the "good practices" of decommodification against those with more disputable social and environmental effects. It is primarily to identify the new levers of social efficacy implemented, as a precondition to the formulation of a decommodification policy – the finality of which would be to decouple social welfare and monetary growth. Consequently, the following developments have a more heuristic purpose than descriptive and analytical.

Emerging practices that can be interpreted as answers to the limits of monetary growth

No human activity is ruled by monetary gains only. The real human individual is never a pure *Homo economicus*, profit is not his/her unique passion and he/she always shares, at least to some extent, the values of his/her social milieu. Only a barely majority part of activities useful to society is carried out for profit. The remaining part – domestic self-production, exchange of services among neighbours, civic and social commitments – amount still to a substantial part of our lives. Besides these ancient forms of social embeddedness of economy, new practices emerge – most often based on a *hybridization between the market logic and the mobilization of non-market resources* – the expansion of which can be seen as an answer to the decline of market economy growth. It seems as if the social development now goes through increased interactions between market sphere and the other spheres of social life.

Social and solidarity economy (SSE): cooperation, co-production and social utility

The SSE takes part in the continuation of long-standing attempts to open a third way between the market and planned economy.[3] The extension of capitalism has generated since the nineteenth century many alternative economic projects, of which the cooperative movement is the most significant and lasting achievement. In parallel, the dynamics of the associative life have counterbalanced the harmful effects of individualism and traditional social solidarity weakening. The SSE is the inheritor of these two movements. It is not a marginal reality: the sector is growing rapidly and represented, in the case of France, more than 10 per cent of employment in 2013. This estimate, however, is somehow misleading, because it corresponds to a broad definition of SSE comprising great firms (for instance cooperative banks), the functioning of which barely differs from that of any great firm. It remains that, even in this enclosing definition, SSE embodies a different vision of economy, with significant impact on the overall system.

The SSE is constituted of two movements, historically distinct: "The first one aggregated under the label social economy cooperatives, mutual insurances, associations and foundations [...] The second movement, which recognized itself in the notion or solidarity economy, is born in later years, in response to the crisis" (Frémeaux 2013: 21). Beyond this historical stratification, these two concepts correspond to two different breaks with the typical model of the capitalist firm.

The main driver of traditional social economy is the will of labour collectives to get emancipated from capitalist domination by their becoming co-owners of the capital. The dependency towards an owner or external investors is "replaced by a financial input of associated members, who get committed because they expect from the activity a service provision and possibly a limited sharing of benefits" (Laville 2010: 229). If it allows the workers to free themselves from capitalist domination, social economy does not seek to break with the market logic. The cooperators produce market goods and face competition like any entrepreneur.

The innovation introduced by the "solidarity economy", as we term it in France, is of another magnitude: beyond the mobilization of social capital for economic purpose, the novelty is about the purposes of organizations and the nature of their production. This new concept appeared in the year 1980 as a response to mass unemployment and, more broadly, to the crisis of social integration through work. The aim is not only to cooperate for a mutual economic benefit, but to contribute to the solving of social problems: "The economic activities are implemented as means to promote democratic and solidarity purposes" (Laville 2010: 255). These purposes set out a plurality of social issues: economic integration, proximity services provision (elder care, etc.), fair trade, development of organic farming, maintenance of local patrimony, etc. It is worth noticing that a 2014 French law states in its first article that a criterion for the belonging of a legal entity to SSE is "a purpose other than benefits sharing". In another article, this purpose is equated to the notion of "social utility", defined by a list of social and environmental objectives (combating social exclusion, energy transition, etc.). This social utility sometimes coincides with a public service mission provided in counterpart of a subvention, but it can result from a social purpose reflecting the particular values of an organization.

We can relate to SSE initiatives aiming to promote ecologically and socially responsible agriculture and healthier food: fair trade, short marketing circuits, shared gardens, urban agriculture, solidarity groceries, etc. They have three types of social finalities: ecological (through cultural practices respectful of environment and the shortening of commercial circuits), social (provide benefits to small producers) and sanitary (healthy food), not forgetting the territorial dimension. Between self-production and proximity trade, the deviation from the market logic are of different magnitude, as well as the involvement of public actors.[4] In all cases, producers and consumers engaged in these experiences have complex motivations, including social ones.

The activity of SSE organizations is doubly integrated in flows of social value, which exceed monetary flows, through its production (social utility) and through the resources it uses. Besides money gained through market activity, these resources include public subsidies and volunteer work. This is called the "hybridization" of resources. Finally, the specificity of SSE organization is reflected by a governance scheme involving different stakeholders (workers, partners, beneficiaries, etc.).

Circular economy: cooperation for resources saving and waste reduction

One of the main drivers of market rationality hybridization is the internalization of environmental constraints, which urges to use more efficiently energy and raw materials. On a finite planet we are not about to leave, all stocks are limited, even those of shale gas. A resource of which consumption grows exponentially (+3.5 per cent annually for iron, for example) will run out sooner or later. In many cases, this will happen within a few decades. Besides, carbonic gas inexorably accumulates, endangering the survival of humankind.

The most appropriate response to these threats consists in the "decoupling"[5] of economic wealth and physical consumption: producing more welfare with less non-renewable resources. A means to achieve this is circular economy, which, as indicated by its name, aims to close the loops of energy and materials. The contribution of Stephan Kampelmann makes it clear that a waste management system calls for an analysis in terms of material flows and social interactions, beyond monetary flows.

In a wider understanding, circular economy goes beyond waste recycling. In order to economize natural resources, one has to optimize their use, reduce induced consumption (energy and consumables), increase their service life, facilitate maintenance and repair, allow the reuse of components and spare parts, and use renewable or easily recycled materials. All these achievements must be facilitated through ecologically oriented product design (eco-design). For example, one of the obstacles to recycling is the use of composite material mixing metals and organic components, which are difficult to separate. Avoiding such situations and allowing the direct reuse of components is one of the core principles of an eco-design approach labelled *Cradle to Cradle*.[6] Another aspect of circular economy is territorial industrial ecology (or industrial symbiosis), namely the organization, at the local level, of cooperation and synergies between nearby firms for optimizing resources use (materials and energy) and waste reuse.

In some ways, circular economy re-engages with ancestral practices. A traditional farm is a perfect example of circular economy: nothing is lost, all is reused or recycled. But the recent developments of circular economy are in no way a return to the past. They may be characterized by a high level of technicality, sophisticated methods and organization devices – with an increasing use of life-cycle assessment (an analysis method of all the environmental impacts generated by the manufacturing, use and scrapping of a product).

The firms which enter the circular economy generally do it for pragmatic reasons of cost-cutting and/or pre-empting future constraints (environmental regulations or physical shortage). One may ask, why can this be termed decommodification? First, because circular economy aims to create utilities (an improvement of the service actually provided by an object over time) and externalities (waste reduction and conservation of scarce resources), the value of which cannot be properly reflected in a market price. More broadly, circular economy entails a revaluation of substantial objectives (ecological and social) to the detriment of pure financial logic. The ecological context forces the firms to define physical targets (reduced energy and material consumption, waste and pollutant effluents reduction) in addition to financial ones. Physical resources shortage as well as new environmental regulations may affect the durability of their business model. Admittedly, the technical rationality has always been a central concern in industry, but it was mostly subsumed in the market rationality;

in other terms, the economic agents express their preferences and constraints through prices only. The novelty of circular economy is that the search for technically and ecologically efficient solutions is becoming a long-term goal in itself, a regulating principle challenging pure financial criteria. Moreover, this principle has a structuring impact on a larger scale, within an industrial sector or a local territory.

At the socio-organizational level, the search for an optimal use of resources requires *more cooperation and predictability*. A more circular economy will be less competing. The firms of a given sector (for example the wood sector) must share the same long-term vision of raw materials stocks (the forests) and cooperate to take up technical challenges and promote recycling activities upstream and downstream of their own activity. This imperative is even more evident in industrial and territorial ecology, which consists in implementing technical long-term partnerships to optimize the use of resources and reuse the waste flows. This cooperation logic, which is the cornerstone of circular economy, is reflected in innovative agreements, which derogate from the rules of competition (Idot 2012). For example, in France, the redemption prices of materials to be recycled (glass, paper and cardboard) are administrative prices. This reinstatement of physical criteria is reflected at the national level in the setting of decoupling objectives, the decoupling ratio between monetary production and physical resources consumption becoming a new criterion for evaluating an economic performance.

From the consumer point of view, *circular economy takes part in self-reliance and monetary needs reduction strategies resulting from the stagnation of the purchasing power, along with the rising of ecological concerns*. This can be seen in the increase of second-hand purchase, the proliferation of *brocantes* and garage sales, as well as of "repair cafés" where people find technical help for repairing goods (there are about ninety in France at present). In this context, it is no surprise that planned obsolescence repression starts being considered. The need of longer lasting and more easily repairable objects stems from financial motives, but not only. It goes along with a greater pragmatism in the evaluation of needs, which are more clearly distinguished from the acquisitive desire,[7] and with a growing rejection of a way of life which makes each individual a significant producer of waste (530 kg for each French person in 2013). The repudiation of the throwaway mentality reflects concerns that are not merely utilitarian, but entail also the aim to live in a cleaner world and a certain notion of culpability towards the wastage of natural resources. This comes to pass through progress in household waste sorting. The free contribution of households to the public service of waste management may be interpreted as a sign of their will to incorporate a civic imperative into their consumption behaviour.

In more systemic terms, it can be said that circular economy recruits all economic agents in cooperative networks about goods and resources, for optimizing their final use and life-cycle. Its development takes part in the progressive distancing of economic reality from the ideal-type of market economy, in which economic agents' cooperation is entirely mediated by commercial exchange.

Functionality economy: from the object to the service and from the service to the solution

To put it simply, functionality economy consists in the replacement of goods ownership by services provided through the use of these goods. The best-known examples are actually little different from classical rental services, except through their public character. The mobility systems such as Paris Vélib and Autolib take part in a rental services growth that benefits commercial services also. Nevertheless, functionality economy can't be reduced to rental services. In some cases at least, other elements must be considered that enrich the concept and increase its innovative character: partnership with territorial communities; users-consumers training; aid in needs analysis and reworking, etc.

The environmental benefits of functionality economy result from both the mutualization of material facilities (allowing to get more service from them) and the fact that the manufacturer, whose financial gains come now from the service provided by the material devices, will find it advantageous to reduce their usage cost (and thus to increase their service life and facilitate their main-tenance).[8] Just as for circular economy, functionality economy contributes to the decoupling between use value and physical flows (energy and material),[9] and thus to the inescapable dematerialization of economy. Beyond the advantage resulting from the optimized use of material resources, the capacity of functionality economy to release ecological constraints stems from its pro-viding of global solutions to complex needs, while bearing positive social externalities. The optimization of the customer/user service profits from co-production effects such as the acquisition of new usage skills and the promoting of more virtuous consumption habits. In this way, Michelin, which has developed a tires rental service for motor carriers, goes further. Beyond the mere rental service, its delivery includes training in eco-driving and mainte-nance (adapted inflation, etc.), in order to reduce the wear and limit fuel con-sumption. Another example is a small manufacturer of video projectors which has shifted towards rental and maintenance service, providing a cost-efficient solution by the way of training users in the competent use of the devices and optimization of their maintenance. In these two cases, the business model is more sophisticated than a mere rental service. The lasting and multidimensional nature of these partnerships draws near to symbiotic relationships.

Collaborative economy: co-production devices with multiple springs

Even though the two terms are often confused, a distinction has to be made between collaborative economy and collaborative consumption, the latter being a subset of the first. Collaborative consumption has pretty much the same effi-ciency levers as functionality economy. Like the latter, it allows a growth of material goods usage value through sharing and cooperation. The main differ-ence between the two stems from their drive: functionality economy generally comes under supply-side initiative (private firms and/or public community), while collaborative economy is more directly based on new consumption practices. There is no clear boundary line, however, as private firms' initiatives tend to influence consumption practices in a proactive way. This can be illustrated by the spectacular success of firms such as Airbnb or Blablacar, a French carpool platform which connects providers and requesters of "seats" on a given route.[10]

Collaborative or sharing economy is a new business fully incorporated in the capitalist economy. Its key players are young creative entrepreneurs, their clients pragmatic consumers seeking to reduce their expenses and goods owners seeking to make money from them. But the decisive factor of this revolution is first and foremost technical: the matching of very specific offers and needs and the drastic reduction of transaction costs have been enabled by the Internet.

So far as they allow to make money with under-utilized goods, rather than freely lending them to family of friends, exchange platforms such as Airbnb or Uber may be seen as typical expressions of a general trend towards commodification, rather than forerunners of a decommodification process. But collaborative consumption practices may also reflect new social attitudes and behaviours, blurring the borderline between monetary and non-monetary social exchange. In the case of Uber at least, there is no shortage of arguments to denounce an unfair competition with taxis. But in other cases, collaborative consumption contributes to a decommodification of lifestyle (barter, exchange of services or apartments, etc.) and may even lead to more creative exchange practices based on reciprocity (collaborative tourism, couchsurfing and colunching).

Anyhow, collaborative consumption always implies a co-production process, and a mixing of the roles of producers and consumers. In this way, it allows a wider valorization of material and social resources. This kind of co-productive activity clearly falls within the concept of decommodification, to the extent that it entails a non-monetary contextualized evaluation of resources and utilities. Market, at least in theory, neutralizes the social context. The famous Adam Smith's statement, "It is not from the benevolence of the butcher, the brewer, or the baker that we expect our dinner," perfectly formulates what the market is supposed to achieve: the autonomy of economic exchange from other dimensions of social life. By contrast, in the collaborative economy, the social relationships quality is intensely and consciously involved as a key production factor. In the examples mentioned above, the importance of the relational factor is admittedly varying, but it remains that both providers and consumers are requested to invest in trustful exchange relations setting. Even when they don't interact face-to-face, they are supposed to belong to the same exchange community, share its norms of reciprocity and even its values. On the Airbnb website, the person who wants to rent an apartment is invited to acquire social know-how and to join a quasi-professional community. The website states:

> Every Airbnb experience is unique and each detail specific to a home, a neighbourhood, and a host. Since our community makes commitments based on these details, we have to be able to trust each other's reliability – whether it be in timely communication, the condition of the home, or in the expectations we set.

The work of the professional broker is partly replaced by the involvement of the renter, and the technical skill of the former by the social skill of the latter – i.e. mainly a capacity to create trust and conviviality. This social resource has a scientific name, social capital, from the eponymous theory of the American sociologist Robert Putnam (Putnam 2000), namely the capacity of social agents to create networks and cooperate for their mutual benefit.

Even though the service is lucrative, it is relevant to refer to decommodification as far as the service quality stems from the mobilizing of a free resource, produced through traders' interaction. The specific productivity lever of the system lies in the activation of social skills by peer-to-peer exchange, which allows transaction costs reductions and a mutualization of know-how about the optimized use of goods. Moreover, peer-to-peer relationships are more easily embedded into a wider scheme of social solidarity and conviviality. Finally, these relationships are supposed to be rewarding. For example, claims such as that are made "the time spent with Uberpop is a convivial time full of anecdotes, in perfect simplicity". This is marketing, admittedly, but it may reflect some reality.

The economic rationality of collaborative consumption stems from a blurring of boundaries between work, consumption, social relations sphere and leisure – a part of what is usually negatively valuated (work) goes to the positive side (personal achievement, autonomy). In terms of externalities, collaborative consumption can be credited with a positive impact on social conviviality, even if the middle classes get more out of it than the poor.[11]

Finally, it should be emphasized that collaborative economy goes well beyond collaborative consumption. It also encompasses, among other emerging activities, crowdfunding and different kinds of collaborative production. These innovations exemplify even more obviously the role played by the Internet as a tool of decommodification. The large-scale networking of personal skills reveals a widespread readiness to cooperate for a joint achievement: "The willingness to make the world better combined to a more widespread distribution of resources to take action, has created a new kind of economic relationship, why not me?" (Colin and Verdier 2012: 85). As noted by these authors, the fact that 80 per cent of contributions to Wikipedia are anonymous shows the existence of a truly disinterested contributive drive.

At first sight, self-production stems from another logic, but, in fact, it is always a cooperative activity. Kitchen gardens and self-housing rehabilitation are informal social answers to the decrease of buying power, but also to the weakening of social links. By the way, their social utility is being recognized by public authorities.

Still few in number (149 worldwide in 2012), fab-labs benefit from the dissemination of 3-D printers. They may prefigure a society of "makers" in which the creation of useful or recreational objects will no longer be the monopoly of industrial firms (Rifkin 2014). All these activities are blurring the boundaries between production, leisure and social life, and thus make still more elusive the concept of economic value.

Decommodification and hybridization within the financial sphere

From the 1980s, the evolution of the economy and finance has been shaped by important reforms whose main consequence has been to increase the power of markets. The 2008 crisis has not made it possible to reverse the trend, but it has cast serious doubt upon the fairness and rationality of the system. Lacking states' clear willingness to recover their regulatory prerogatives, different social actors have taken over to try and submit finance to social aims.

Within corporate social and environmental responsibility approaches, social and environmental data complement the financial reporting. The aim is to evaluate firms, taking into account all the impacts of their activity. Socially responsible investment (SRI) belongs to the same approach, implemented through savers' decisions. In their own way, these practices fall within the concept of decommodification, in the sense of limitation of the market's evaluating and prescribing power. In spite of the legitimate suspicion inspired by corporate communication (too often leading to mere greenwashing), they may reflect and accompany real changes in corporate culture, up to the point of making less clear-cut the distinction between ordinary firms and those belonging to social and solidarity economy (Frémeaux 2013: 23).

However, the effect of these correctives on the functioning of the economic system remains marginal; they have little weight against corporate greed. The financial system functioning requires wider reforms, with two objectives: first, acknowledge and institute the social missions of the firm, and second, facilitate long-term investments (especially those needed by the ecological transition). Accordingly, it is worth noting the emergence of reflections about the institutionalization, or even "constitutionalization" of the firm, based on legal arguments contradicting the neoliberal approach (Robé 2014: 23). A research team has recently proposed to create an "extended social purpose firm" status, whose provisions would be opposable to the shareholders (Levillain *et al.* 2014). Such an innovation could have so much more impact that other regulating policy measures would be taken simultaneously, in order to limit the market's power in savings allocation and the evaluation of firms, currencies and financial assets. In that respect, André Orléan evokes a "de-financialization" consisting of "the creation of an evaluating power independent from financial markets, that would take into account projects consistent with general interest" (Orléan 2012). Inspired by similar considerations, banking reform projects currently in debate would reduce the amount of speculative funds through the separation of deposit bank activity from investment bank activity.[12] These ideas stem from similar intentions: institute the firm as a collective creation project and limit the market's power over savings allocation.

Complementary local currencies are another hybridization strategy, based upon the creation of new exchange mediums dedicated to specific uses related to social purposes. They constitute another facet of the multidimensional answer to the loss of economic growth social efficiency. According to Bernard

Lietaer (2008), more than 4,000 such currencies exist worldwide (about 100 in 1990), including dozens in France. Although these numbers seem important, the practical impact of this movement remains very small: most of counted initiatives are ephemeral and of limited size, and their vitality depends entirely on associative militancy.[13] However, the 2014 French legislation on social and solidarity economy gives a legal status to local currencies, bringing evidence that the subject is not merely anecdotal. The general concept is that of an exchange tool partially convertible in national (or European) currency, for specific commercial use related to solidarity enforcement within a local territory (Lietaer 2008). In summary, these currencies "allow a relocation of economic activities by an earmarking of monetary flows" (Ragot 2014).[14] Because they don't allow for interest-bearing loans or for investment financing (some of them are "smelting", their value decreasing over time when they don't circulate),[15] they don't create financial activities, which is an assumed limitation. Hence, they always live in symbiosis with a fully convertible currency. It is unlikely that these experiments spread spontaneously, but they are nonetheless significant forerunners of new social change strategies. For example, a complementary currency could be used by a state as a means to create or redistribute buying power dedicated to high-priority social needs' fulfilment (it is already the case for some existing social policy tools such as vouchers or Checks for Universal Employment Services (CESU) in France). Put at the service of a social project, monetary pluralism could constitute a powerful lever of social change.

Decommodification as a social development strategy

The hypothesis discussed a bit further in my book is that all these innovations – especially hybrid activities combining market and non-market mechanisms – bring conceptual bricks needed to build a decommodification strategy, which is the only path towards a decoupling of social welfare and market growth. For improving social welfare with a low or zero economic growth, there is no other solution than reducing monetary needs and intensifying non-monetary values flows.

Besides the supporting of decommodification practices such as those described above, a social development strategy based upon a zero-growth premise should bear policy measures aiming for such objectives as:

- extend the lifespan of goods (through technical norms and regulations);
- help households, particularly those with weak resources, to reduce their expenses without degrading their living conditions (information for consumers on goods usage cost, water and energy supply progressive pricing, living without car facilitation through urban planning and collective transport promotion, etc.);
- limit the cost and nuisance of unsolicited advertising (possibly prohibit unsolicited mailing advertising).

The public sector could contribute in different ways to the reduction of material consumption and to the mutualization of goods. Its size allows a significant impact on productive supply and social practices, be it through procurement policy, public decisions evaluation criteria or free use of public equipment by civil society organizations.

Finally, let's recognize that these measures would leave unsolved a major question: a decommodification strategy would weigh negatively on fiscal resources and result in a reducing of public policy means. The only coherent answer to this challenge would be to *demonetarize the public service itself (at least a part of it)*. That is, concretely, answer to collective needs through other means than public job creation. Beyond the issue of civic service (whose revival is periodically considered in France), this points to the development of a collaborative civil service relying on the citizens' propensity to freely contribute to the common good.

Obviously, the implementation of these decommodification measures could greatly benefit from a work organization allowing a differentiated use of lifetime. Within the framework of *ecology of social time*, issues such as the transition between work and inactivity – including the promotion of volunteer activity of retirees – should notably be considered.

None of this is entirely new. Most often, however, measures of this kind play a marginal role in public policies and policy debates. They are considered secondary compared to measures with a strong financial impact (taxation, subsidies, investments, etc.). The novelty of my proposal lies in a change in perspective: all the measures listed above could help to disconnect social welfare from economic growth. At the political level, going in this direction would require improvements in the way democracy works (co-construction of public policies, participative democratic governance of commons, citizens' education and empowerment for increasing their capacity to take into account the non-monetary in decisions and negotiation processes). Within such a perspective, the measures outlined above could be the levers of a global transformation of the economic system and society.

Notes

1 This chapter consists for the most part of Chapter 3 of this book.
2 Let's remember that, for Esping-Andersen (1990), decommodification refers to the reduction of the individual's dependency towards the market thanks to the welfare system.
3 In France, a law voted in 2014 has given a unified legal framework to the SSE sector.
4 A 2010 European study shows an "omnipresence of the public actor", in contrast to the United States where short circuits are most often "alternative systems with a marginal and militant character". The study shows that

> 110 initiatives or types of initiatives have been identified throughout EU. Four types of organizations appear: consumers becoming producers, lasting partnership between farmers and consumers, direct sales on local markets, sales via local commerce; and two main objectives: the establishment of stable relationships or occasional commercial outlet.

> (Gassie 2014)

5 "Decoupling" is measured by several indicators of resource productivity. One of them is the GDP divided by an aggregated indicator of resources consumption. Its growth rate has been about 30 per cent since 1990, which is seriously inadequate (so much more that it does not take into account the material consumption generated by imported products).

6 Referring to the book of Michael Braungart and William McDonough (2002).

7 As quoted in CREDOC (2013: 52): "the satisfaction of needs is less anchored in the material".

8 In this way, thanks to its sales system of a photocopying service (as an alternative to photocopier sales), Xerox evaluates the annual reduction of CO_2 emissions to be 600,000 tons (Teulon 2014).

9 By the way, functionality economy is sometimes seen a subset of circular economy.

10 The firm is active in 190 countries and generates annual incomes estimated at \$120 millions in 2012. As an illustration of its growth, the website indicates that "350 000 travelers have already stayed in France with Airbnb, of which 80% these 12 last months".

11 According to a 2013 study, 68.5 per cent of people practising car-sharing have higher qualifications. Nothing mysterious in that: people with higher social and cultural capital find it easier to participate in an exchange network (Godillon and Louvet 2013). But care must be taken in making generalizations: disadvantaged people are the main beneficiaries of barter and second-hand sales growth. Moreover, the tenuous links between collaborative economy and SSE might develop.

12 This refers to the 2013 banking regulation in France and to the related debates.

13 According to a French official report (Magnen *et al.* 2015), the average money stock is about 26,000 euro.

14 Anne-Cécile Ragot quoted by the daily *La Croix*, 15 May 2014.

15 Thus, "l'abeille" (the honeybee) in the town of Villeneuve-sur-Lot loses 2 per cent of its value every six months.

References

Braungart, M. and McDonough, W. (2002). *Cradle to Cradle: Remaking the Way We Make Things*. New York: North Point Press.

Colin, N. and Verdier, H. (2012). *L'âge de la multitude: entreprendre et gouverner après la révolution numérique*. Paris: Armand Colin.

CREDOC (2013). Va-t-on vers une frugalité choisie? *Cahiers de recherche*, December.

Esping-Andersen, G. (1990). *The Three Worlds of Welfare Capitalism*. Princeton: Princeton University Press.

Frémeaux, P. (2013). *L'évaluation de l'apport de l'économie sociale et solidaire*. Rapport au ministre Benoît Hamon.

Gassie, J. (2014). La dimension territoriale des circuits courts. *Bulletin de veille du centre de prospective du ministère de l'Agriculture*, November.

Godillon, S. and Louvet, N. (2013). *Enquête nationale sur l'autopartage*. Cabinet 6T et ADEME.

Idot, L. (2012). Droit de la concurrence et protection de l'environnement. *Concurrences*, 3.

Laville, J.-L. (2010). *Politique de l'association*. Paris: Seuil.

Levillain, K., Hatchuel, A. and Segrestin, B. (2014). Normer l'entreprise pour l'émanciper? Vers de nouvelles options juridiques. In B. Segrestin, B. Roger and S. Vernac (eds), *L'entreprise, point aveugle du savoir, Actes du colloque de Cerisy*. Paris: Éditions Sciences humaines, pp. 315–330.

Lietaer, B. (2008). *Monnaies régionales: de nouvelles voies vers une prospérité durable.* Paris: Fondation Charles-Léopold Meyer.

Magnen, J.-P., Fourel, C. and Meunier, N. (2015). D'autres monnaies pour une nouvelle prospérité, Rapport remis à Carole Delga, Secrétaire d'État chargée du commerce, de l'artisanat, de la consommation et de l'économie sociale et solidaire le 8 avril 2015.

Orléan, A. (2012). Pour une approche alternative de l'économie, entretien avec Olivier Mongin et Clémence Lalaut. *Esprit*, February: 111–129.

Perret, B. (2015). *Au-delà du marché. Les nouvelles voies de la démarchandisation.* Paris: Les Petits Matins et Institut Veblen.

Putnam, R. (2000). *Bowling Alone: Collapse and Revival of American Community.* New York: Simon & Schuster.

Ragot, A.-C. (2014). Quoted in *La Croix*, 15 May.

Rifkin, J. (2014). *The Zero Marginal Cost Society: The Internet of Things, the Collaborative Commons, and the Eclipse of Capitalism.* Palgrave Macmillan.

Robé, J.-P. (2014). Comment s'assurer que les entreprises respectent l'intérêt général. *L'Économie politique*, 64: 22–35.

Teulon, H. (2014). *Le guide de l'éco-innovation.* Paris: ADEME/Eyrolles.

4　Social economy and polycentric governance of transitions

Thomas Bauwens and Sybille Mertens

The transition[1] to socio-economic systems that would both break away from the ideology of growth and be socially and environmentally sustainable is dependent on transformations that themselves require a coordinated effort by society as a whole and an increased sense of responsibility on the part of all the actors that constitute it (i.e. public authorities, firms, consumers and civil society). Representative examples of the challenges we face collectively include: the fight against climate change, the protection of biodiversity, the regulation of the global financial system, the preservation of social cohesion, the eradication of poverty, and the fight against socio-economic inequalities. Such a transition thus entails numerous problems with regard to collective action. In economic terms, collective action refers to any activity that requires the coordination of two or more individuals. This coordination, however, is not self-evident: according to conventional economic theory, in the context of providing public goods, rational individuals who pursue their individual interests have incentives to behave as "free riders" and to rely on the contributions of others without bearing their share of the costs of these provisions (Olson 1965). It is for this reason that the market does not offer an adequate institutional framework for the provision of public goods (Samuelson 1954).

What institutions then must be established in order to create and support the necessary collective actions? The market's inability to provide public goods has frequently served as a justification for government action to carry out this function. From this perspective, the social and ecological transition doubtless requires some guidance to coordinate the overall movement and to define (democratically legitimate) macro-economic goals. Public decision-makers are in a privileged position to assume this role with the aid of appropriate tools such as the alternative indicators to gross domestic product that Thiry presents elsewhere in this volume.

It would be unrealistic and counterproductive, however, to think that this transition could be entirely steered from the top down. National governments cannot face all of the challenges posed by the transition alone, as it is a complex process that involves a multitude of interconnected issues and involves a myriad of very different actors. It therefore appears necessary to draw on the resources and knowledge of non-state actors situated at more decentralized levels of governance. These non-state actors may prove essential to solving problems encountered on the ground and to establishing sustainable initiatives that are adapted to local realities.

In the literature on collective action, those systems of governance that combine many decision-making centres corresponding to multiple levels of jurisdiction – local, provincial, regional, national and global – and that are formally independent of one another are called "polycentric" systems, as opposed to "monocentric" systems, which imply a single decision-making centre and a single level of governance (Ostrom *et al.* 1961).

A key assumption to polycentric approaches is that governance arrangements are more effective when citizens are able to get involved in the decision-making process by means of self-organization (Andersson and Ostrom 2008). This chapter focuses on initiatives that begin within civil society and that claim no association with the two well-known coordinating mechanisms of state authority and the direct and exclusive recourse to market transactions.

While citizen involvement and the ability of citizens to self-organize both prove necessary to the transition, the types of organizations that appear suited to fill this role and to guide citizen action have received little scholarly attention, at least in regard to their connection to the transition. This prospective chapter thus aims to fill the gap and to explore the roles that social economy organizations[2] can play in the polycentric governance of the socio-ecological transition. We posit that their specific organizational modalities make these organizations particularly well-suited to guide self-organized citizen action and thus favour the development of polycentric systems. The use of these structures could, in turn, catalyse the gradual emergence of a post-growth paradigm.

This chapter is composed of five sections. In the first section, we establish a connection between the nature of the goods to be produced in a transition perspective and the problems this poses in regard to collective action. In the second section, we develop the concept of polycentric governance. The third section then describes the dynamics of self-organization and the modes of coordination they entail. In the fourth section, we use the literature on the organizational forms of social economy to cast light on their potential roles in providing a framework for these self-organized initiatives and then examine their ability to support the progressive development of a post-growth paradigm. In the fifth section, we illustrate the pertinence of our proposition by applying this interpretive framework to the energy and food sectors.

The nature of goods and the problems of collective action

Following Samuelson (1954), economic goods are often classified into two categories: public goods and private goods. A good is private when its consumer captures all the benefits connected to its consumption. A public good, however, is characterized by non-rivalry and non-excludability. Non-excludability means that it is difficult to exclude individuals who have not paid for the consumption of a good, while non-rivalry means that the consumption of a good by one individual does not limit the consumption of this same good by others. Determining the "public" value of a good, however, is quite difficult, especially as rivalry and excludability are rarely discrete categories; that is to say, few goods are completely (non-)rivalrous or totally (non-)exclusive. These attributes define a *spectrum* of situations rather than pure categories. As such, many goods have both private and public characteristics. These goods, qualified here as "semi-public", are private goods whose use generates externalities. Let us take two examples that we will continue to discuss later in the chapter: the consumption of electricity produced by sources of renewable energy generates private benefits for the consumer (the consumption of electricity), but also has positive effects for the general public (it increases the capacity for renewable energy, reduces greenhouse gases associated with conventional energy sources, creates work in the renewable energy industry, decreases dependence on imported resources, etc.). Similarly, the consumption of seasonal food products in a short distribution channel is a source of private utility for consumers as well as generating positive effects on public goods (reinforced food safety, reduction of certain adverse environmental impacts, etc.).

The production of public and semi-public goods naturally leads to the free rider problem. Indeed, non-exclusion (directly related to the consumption of the good in the first case and indirectly related to it through the enjoyment of positive externalities in the second case) poses the threat of underproduction because those who benefit from the collective positive effects related to the existence of these goods are not encouraged to contribute to the financing of their production as they are certain not to be excluded. Consequently, producing public goods and seeking to integrate the collective (social and environmental) impacts of our economic actions into our individual choices requires individual actions to be coordinated by other mechanisms than those of the market, as these lead to sub-optimal results. The state is traditionally expected to coordinate collective action; but more recently, in view of the magnitude of the challenges and the limits of centralized state action, a literature has developed around the notion of a polycentric system of governance.

The necessity of a polycentric transition

Polycentric systems of governance are receiving increasing attention in relation to the establishment of a governance regime for complex collective action situations (Aligica and Tarko 2012). These systems can be described as the combination of many decision-making centres corresponding to multiple levels of jurisdiction – local, provincial, regional, national and global – that are formally independent of one another and that operate according to a set of common rules (Ostrom *et al.* 1961).

The notion of polycentric governance is based on two key ideas: first, the pertinence of localism, and second, the capacity of actors to self-organize. As regards the first idea, local transition actions prove crucial to solving problems of collective action. For instance, Ostrom (2010) suggests that, contrary to the widespread view that global issues can only be resolved at a global level, local initiatives play an important role in providing global public goods, such as in the fight against climate change or the preservation of biodiversity.

The second fundamental postulate of polycentric approaches is that governance arrangements are more effective when citizens have the legal and material capacities to self-organize multiple governing bodies at different levels (Andersson and Ostrom 2008). The concept of self-organization is grounded in the idea that events and actions do not necessarily require an external stimulus or a hierarchically superior force in order to take place – they can arise from internal causes driven by endogenous dynamics. It is from this view that Ostrom (1990) seeks to construct a theory of collective action that could account for human endeavours in which the individuals involved organize themselves on a voluntary basis to overcome the free rider problem (especially on the basis of norms of reciprocity and cooperation).

Economists traditionally believe, on the contrary, that this phenomenon can only be overcome by an external solution, provided either by the state – through the establishment of regulatory standards or the introduction of a Pigovian tax[3] – or by the market – through the establishment of a system of individual property rights, according to the Coase theorem. Rejecting this alternative, Ostrom (1990) ventures to demonstrate the existence of a third economically efficient coordinating mechanism – the management of collective goods by the communities themselves, through the establishment of "institutional arrangements". It is especially important that it be the community's drive to resolve their direct problems that defines the creation of these arrangements, as this is an essential condition for the sustainability of these processes.

The original justification for polycentric systems was a normative one: it was based on the belief that any collective problem should be solved as locally as possible – by the level of governance capable of dealing with it that would be closest to the individual – according to a principle of subsidiarity. It is now widely accepted that the polycentric governance of complex institutional systems has practical advantages over highly centralized systems. First, polycentric systems have informational advantages in that they encourage the use of local knowledge to design rules that are better suited to the locale than a set of general rules. Second, general governing of collective actions would require the establishment of highly complex rule systems such that no expert could fully analyse them. Third, the local beneficiaries of collective approaches know one another; they are thus in a better position to select partners who are trustworthy and to exclude those who are not, thereby improving the conditions for cooperation and reciprocity among participants. Fourth, polycentricity reinforces the system's resilience – its capacity to absorb a shock or disturbance. Indeed, by creating redundancy through the multiplicity of local decision-making centres, it strengthens the conditions for experimentation and creativity necessary for exploring new combinations of potentially superior rule systems. Finally, polycentricity reduces the cost of applying common rules, reinforcing their legitimacy as a result of their local anchoring.

In short, the polycentric solution to the dilemma of collective action consists in breaking down a global challenge into a number of smaller scale problems that are more easily overcome, especially thanks to a higher pre-existing level of trust between participants. Polycentricity should not, however, be confused with a completely decentralized system of governance. Indeed, decentralization does not always amount to the emergence of a self-organized system. Without an institutional and cultural framework to structure overall coordination, the governance regime risks becoming nothing more than an agglomeration of fragmented initiatives. Top-down institutional initiatives are thus just as necessary to the sustainability of a polycentric system as those actions initiated from the bottom; they must notably ensure overall coordination and the resolution of conflicts, facilitate the mobilization of sufficient resources for larger issues, and divide up the costs of self-organization more equitably between different communities.

The dynamics of self-organization

The self-organized citizens' projects on which polycentric systems partially depend are not static constructions, but dynamic processes that go through various stages of development. Though we will not go into a detailed description of these stages, it is useful to distinguish the launch phase of an initiative from the subsequent development phases, especially because they often involve different funding mechanisms. Similarly, we may identify two groups of actors with different motivations associated with these two phases: "founders" and "late joiners".

The launch phase generally takes place in what the transition studies literature calls a "niche" environment (Kemp *et al.* 1998), which is to say, a space isolated from the selective pressures of the market in which technical and social innovations may develop. As such, initiatives mostly rely on voluntary resources and sometimes on public resources (e.g. pilot projects).

While not all citizens' initiatives necessarily seek to expand, the development of certain organizations' activities is generally explained by two factors. First, development is a strategy to limit the risks of running out of steam, which can affect initiatives that rely almost entirely on the motivation of its founders and on their voluntary contributions of resources. Slowdown occurs when the people carrying the project feel they are victim to free riders. They realize that their great efforts generate positive effects for the collectivity and desire a larger contributor base to provide these efforts (Mertens 2010). Second, the development of activities is supported by the growing reputation of the initiative, which gains legitimacy and attracts the attention of public authorities and individuals with similar motivations to those of the founders. A ramp up is often to be expected in these cases, and the organization gradually leaves its initial niche environment.

An activity's development also occasions its first internal tensions, or "endogenous" limits of self-organization. One major tension resides in the well-known negotiation between scaling and preserving initial values. Initiatives that decide to widen their fields of action often adopt a logic of "hybridization" by which they combine their initial logics with certain leading practices. For example, in order to attract more members or to mobilize additional resources, initiatives frequently offer members the possibility to obtain tangible private benefits from their participation. The initial voluntary resources thus gradually give way to commercial resources, justified by the private benefits received by members. Initiatives often gain the ability to receiving public funding at this same time, either because public authorities consider the organization to be worthy of carrying out certain tasks or because the organization has succeeded in mobilizing public opinion, which has in turn found a voice in political decisions. Here again we observe a hybridization of logics: a citizen-based approach built on voluntary resources becomes a collaboration with the state, which institutionalizes the basis of collective funding. We can also see this movement towards the hybridization of institutional logics at the membership level, where a second category of member appears, and which we can qualify as "late joiners". Those who join the project in later development phases have various motivations for doing so, such as a diminished perception of risks associated with the launch phase or the introduction of private benefits connected to participation.

The transformation that occurs at this stage brings with it a significant risk of institutional isomorphism if left unchecked. We may define this risk as the tendency of organizations active in the same field to resemble one another and to conform to a dominant model (DiMaggio and Powell 1983). Organizations come to adopt the codes and conduct of the institutions in their field both for reasons of legitimacy and due to their dependence on new sources of income. While market financing may lead a citizens' organization to imitate the practices of its competition, even unintentionally ("competition" understood here as those who offer the same kind of private benefits), so too does public funding – which is generally accompanied by a significant degree of control (accreditation, regulatory framework, etc.) – lead to a standardization of the organizations receiving funding. Though a citizens' initiative is initially distinguished by its innovation, it can quickly pay the price of institutional recognition by becoming a mere appendage of the state.

Beyond the endogenous limits set out above, the room these initiatives have to manoeuvre is also circumscribed by "exogenous" limits to self-organization. Indeed, they emerge and evolve in a pre-established context with physical and institutional constraints. The empirical domains in which social and ecological transactions are particularly urgent in view of the contemporary social and environmental challenges (transportation, energy production, agri-food sector) are distinguished by centralized configurations, multiple "socio-technical locks-in" (Maréchal 2010), and dominant firms in positions of strength comparative to new arrivals. Despite the temporary protection of the niches mentioned above, these contexts constrain self-organizing actors.

The role of social economy organizations in providing frameworks for self-organized initiatives

Considering what role self-organized initiatives might play in a polycentric transition system requires that we think about the organizational models best suited to them. Two kinds of model appear especially pertinent: cooperatives and associations. First, we will reflect on the specificities of different organizational structures (what they allow for in terms of polycentric governance and social and ecological transition). We will then complete this organizational analysis by turning our attention to the individual level.

Fitting organizational forms: cooperatives and associations

Citizens generally make use of organizational forms that are more broadly cate-gorized as social economy organizations (Defourny and Develtere 2000); these range from associative to cooperative to mutualist models that have been specifi-cally conceived from the outset to enable groups of people (most often physical people, but sometimes moral persons as well) to work together in the pursuit of goals that could be qualified as "non-capitalist". The common goal of these citizens is not the enrichment of those who contribute capital – rather they work together to find collective solutions to their needs or to those of the community to which they belong. This approach does not exclude the possibility for members to reap material or immaterial benefits, but the benefits generated are primarily directed towards the public. We find examples of local collective actions undertaken by citizens using these organizational forms in fields as varied as energy, food, finance and transportation.

Before venturing further, it is important to note that in favouring the pursuit of a finality of service to their members or to the collectivity rather than a finality of profit, these organizational forms exceed the Friedmanian view of firms (Friedman 1970). This stance proves to be extremely useful in a post-growth economy. Indeed, as Méda underscores elsewhere in this volume, the overall goal of eco-nomic growth is associated, on the microeconomic level, with a logic of profit maximization for capital, often at the expense of social or environmental matters. Conversely, it is probable that in a post-growth economy, the maximization of profitability will no longer be a firm's primary driver. As Perret asserts in this volume, the economic models implemented in the context of social economy show that taking distance from the ultimate aim of profitability for the shareholder creates room to promote economic activities that optimize the positive effects on the collectivity in terms of social cohesion, equity and environmental protection. This is not to say that social economy organizations are the only ones able to avoid the exclusive pursuit of maximum profitability, but the institutional characteristics of social economy organizations do offer more credible guarantees in regard to the pursuit of collective goals as compared to conventional firms.

These guarantees mainly consist of non-capitalist ownership regimes. Owner-ship is traditionally defined according to the assignment of two rights: the right to residual surplus and the residual right of control (Milgrom and Roberts 1992). In a capitalist firm, ownership belongs to those who provide the capital; they are granted these rights in proportion to their contribution to the company's capital. In citizen-based initiatives that take an associative or a cooperative form, ownership is not granted to investors. In associations, ownership rights are allocated weakly: first, strictly speaking, there is no holder of the right to residual surplus. Second, rights of control are granted to members of the association on a democratic basis. In a cooperative model, ownership belongs, in principle, to "user members". This notion refers to the double identity of the members of these organizations: they are both members (who provide capital) and users (who use the organization's services). In other words, investing in these organizations is not enough to attain the status of owner and to enjoy joint rights of ownership; ownership rights are granted to members in their role as users rather than as providers of capital. When a cooperative is used by a citizens' initiative that seeks to produce public or semi-public goods, the founding members are not always users (in the sense of consumers of private goods, workers, or suppliers through the cooperative). However, when these initiatives combine private incentives with participation, the members who benefit from them possess this double identity.

What do these two forms of ownership that are distinct from capitalist ownership enable? The neo-institutional economic literature on not-for-profits (Anheier and Ben-Ner 2002; Hansmann 1996; Steinberg 2006) allows us to argue that they provide important advantages for resolving two problems that naturally arise when considering collective action: the state's failure to provide enough public goods and the problems of imperfect information.

On the one hand, when collective action is in the hands of public authorities, the leadership's choices regarding the public production of collective services (the quantity of services to produce, the quality of these services, and the share of the public budget allotted to them) are carried out in accordance with the wishes of the median voter per the Hotelling-Downs model (Downs 1957), favouring the most influential voter groups and neglecting the issues whose effects only concern minorities or which are mainly local (Santos 2012). Private not-for-profit organizations often emerge in places where the state's collective action is judged by certain citizens to be insufficient in quantity or quality (Weisbrod 1975). The private and democratic character of these organizations enables citizens in proximity to the needs they seek to satisfy to gather freely with the simple shared desire to find a common solution.

On the other hand, collective action requires the mobilization of individual resources in order to formulate an answer to a collective need. This mobilization of resources is only possible if the members and, more broadly, the resource providers see the organizational form as a vehicle capable of establishing a level of trust and of avoiding (or strongly reducing) the risks of opportunistic behaviour associated with imperfect information. These risks are of two kinds:

1   the free rider phenomenon; and
2   information asymmetries related to the production of credence goods.

First, cooperatives and associations seem to be capable of providing an organizational answer to the free rider problem mentioned above. In order to establish a level of trust and to encourage the adoption of cooperative strategies, it is essential that the actors involved in the production of collective goods have information about the other individuals with whom they interact. Specifically, they should ensure that each individual shares the extra-economic motivations inherent to this kind of activity. In this context, other than the small size of the groups that facilitate personal interactions, the constraint of the non-redistribution of surpluses within associations or of its limitation within cooperatives acts as a "selection" mechanism; it is a guarantee against potential investors whose sole motivation is profit and attracts workers whose goals and values are in alignment with the organization's mission of general interest (Rose-Ackerman 1996). Other norms, such as social identification with the group, often develop within social economy organizations. Indeed, voluntary involvement in a group pursuing an explicit common objective creates a feeling of belonging that leads participants to contribute to the group's success (Tyler and Blader 2001).

Second, if a collective action generates information asymmetries, resource providers may fear that the organization in charge of the collective action uses its informational advantage to the detriment of other parties, by offering an inferior quality of product that reduces production costs or simply by placing an excessive price on the goods or services produced. According to Hansmann (1980), an associative organization that explicitly champions a non-capitalist finality and that also subjects itself to a non-distribution constraint seems more trustworthy than a conventional firm because it has fewer incentives to exploit informational problems in order to reduce the quality of its product or service. Spear (2000) and Hansmann (1996) use the same argument in the case of cooperatives. The limitation of the distribution of profits acts as a signal of trust because it limits the incentives for the organization or those who run it to behave opportunistically. In theory, then, the non-distribution constraint is sufficient to guarantee the pursuit of the collective interest. In practice, however, this provision may be circumvented in a variety of ways through the adoption of implicit forms of redistribution. In this context, and beyond the inherent value they may present, democratic management and the participatory dynamic that it underpins allow members to exercise internal control over the quality of production and to reinforce the level of trust within an organization.

Trust thus constitutes a central element in facilitating the mobilization of resources for collective action. It is indispensable for trust to exist between members as well as between the organization and other potential resource providers. It is no small feat to create a climate of trust within a group, as trust is itself a collective good and thus constitutes a second-order dilemma (Marshall 2005). This dilemma may be overcome through norms of reciprocity. As we have seen above, cooperatives and associations present institutional characteristics likely to facilitate the emergence of such norms. Yet the adoption and reinforcement of rules that favour these reciprocal strategies are themselves collective goods and thus imply a third-order dilemma. In this paradox, the question that remains to be resolved is: how it is possible in the first place to generate a sufficient level of trust that leads certain individuals to get involved in such initiatives? The answer lies partly in the motivations and preferences of these individuals.

Implications on the individual level

These organization-level considerations are only meaningful if one accepts their implications on the individual level. Indeed, giving citizens a role in a polycentric system makes it necessary to examine their ability and motivation as economic agents to set up and to interact effectively with such organizational forms. In particular, we must seek to better understand how the resources and aspirations of individuals resonate with certain organizational forms and/or how these forms are made possible and sustainable by factors pertaining to the individual. This exercise implicitly leads us to recognize the diversity of individual motivations that underpin economic activities beyond the supposed universality of the rational maximization of individual utility. The study of these motivations in the context of social economy organizations highlights two particularly interesting points.

First, rather than assembling a collection of disparate individuals, social economy organizations are most often built up from pre-existing social networks (Granovetter 1973). Social economy initiatives – indeed, all economic activities, broadly speaking – do not materialize in a social vacuum, but are embedded in pre-established belief and norm systems. The actors that make up these organizations form communities based on geography or interest (they live in the same neighbourhood, have worked in the same company, belong to the same religious community, share similar political or ideological positions, etc.) and are united by the idea of facing the socio-economic problems with which they are confronted in solidarity.

Second, psychological studies have demonstrated that even in the absence of these pre-existing social relationships, economic actors can be intrinsically motivated to engage in such activities (Frey 1997). In other words, they undertake tasks for the sake of the tasks themselves and the inherent satisfaction they derive from them rather than for external factors such as financial gain. Benz (2005), for example, uses data gathered from the United States and the United Kingdom during the 1990s to show that non-profit workers are generally more satisfied with their work than their counterparts in the for-profit sector – an observation that can be attributed to non-monetary motivations but not to wage differences. Other studies establish positive correlations between the level of intrinsic motivation within cooperatives and associations on the one hand and job satisfaction and productivity on the other (Becchetti *et al.* 2013; Borzaga and Tortia 2006).

Two examples: the energy and agri-food industries

Let us illustrate our point by taking for example the energy and agri-food indus-tries. These industries are each confronted with different general issues, but among those issues that affect both of them, climate change is doubtless one of the most worrisome. Both industries also face more specific threats to energy security and food security respectively: take for example the depletion of non-renewable resources (oil for the energy sector, phosphate for agriculture, and gas reserves for both sectors) or the depletion of fresh water and the destruction of soils and wetlands for agriculture. All of these fundamentally interconnected issues have in common the fact that they transcend national borders while affect-ing the well-being of all.

It is for this reason that many analysts argue for an institutional solution to be negotiated at the international level. International negotiations, however, are slow and often of limited efficiency because, as states defend their divergent interests, negotiations often only result in declarations of good intentions or, at best, unambitious treaties. If local actors wait for an international agreement to be reached before taking action, they risk losing numerous opportunities to take positive action at smaller scales. Climate change, for example, is the result of a myriad of activities developed by individuals, households and firms at much more local levels. A global solution can only be implemented effectively if all of these actors change their behaviour.

Acting at the local level, however, is not a simple task. The socio-technical configurations of the two sectors considered here have long since excluded citizen participation. The dominant energy infrastructure model is characterized by large thermal power stations generally situated near sources of fossil fuels and kept far from sites of consumption; its end users are thus involved very little in the process of energy production. Following this same logic, the industrial agri-food system has favoured the development of an agriculture that is heavily dependent on international markets in terms of both input (e.g. fertilizers created from petrochemicals) and output (the products sold). This trajectory has led to a disconnect between producers and consumers as well as to a food supply of questionable quality.

However, things may well be changing. In recent years, collective dynamics seeking a citizens' reappropriation of economic activities have been emerging in both energy and agri-food sectors. In the energy sector, renewable energies such as photovoltaic panels and onshore wind turbines enable decentralized energy production with small production units that are geographically dis-persed and situated near users. This frees consumers from the electric grid to a certain degree and allows them to choose their energy source. In the agri-food sector, a series of alternative networks – most commonly initiated by civil society – are attempting to restore direct and congenial relationships between consumers and producers. In seeking to shorten food supply chains, these initi-atives strive to both guarantee fair payment to producers and to assure customers of food quality.

Social economy organizations offer ideal organizational forms to frame such citizen engagement. In the energy sector, the rise of decentralized energy production has been accompanied by the emergence of renewable energy cooperatives (Bauwens 2016; Bauwens *et al.* 2016; Huybrechts and Mertens 2014). These organizations offer citizens an opportunity to become owners of their own renewable energy generating units (solar panels, wind turbines, small hydroelectric installations, etc.) installed in their surroundings. They thereby become direct recipients of the economic benefits created by energy generation as well as becoming involved in decision-making processes. Thanks to these characteristics and to the establishment of a level of trust with developers, participation in a cooperative significantly increases the positive attitude towards controversial technologies such as onshore wind turbines (Bauwens 2015). Cooperatives also mobilize financial resources and social capital in order to set up other sustainable energy projects beyond energy generation, relying on both monetary incentives and social norms among members (Bauwens 2016). Thus, thanks to the level of trust established with their members and the activation of social norms, these organizations also occupy a privileged place in the implementation of projects targeting energy efficiency and the reduction of energy consumption per capita. Compared to energy production (renewable or not), this last point is absolutely crucial in the context of a post-growth economy. As such, these organizations often include support for measures that aim to reduce the consumption of their members as part of their mission – this being in the interest of the consumers who control the organization (Bauwens and Eyre 2017). For example, Connexus Energy, Minnesota's largest cooperative energy provider, which supplies electricity to approximately 125,000 households, teamed up with Opower to launch one of the longest-running behaviour-based energy efficiency programmes in the United States. Reports containing analyses of household energy usage, comparisons with neighbouring households, and advice on saving energy were sent to members and a web portal was created. The programme achieved energy savings of over 2 per cent in six months. During the first three years of the programme, Connexus households have collectively reduced their consumption by approximately 30,000 MWh and have thereby avoided producing CO_2 emissions equivalent to 350 internal airline flights (Laskey and Syler 2013).

Localized alternative agri-food networks seeking to promote socioenvironmental finalities also tend to borrow structures from social economy: take for example producer cooperatives oriented towards social finalities, mixed producer and consumer cooperatives, and joint purchasing groups. A closer look at these initiatives allows us to highlight the advantages of organizational models proposed by social economy, both in terms of their pertinence in guiding citizens' initiatives and their ability to gradually transform the behaviour of initiative participants (Seyfang 2006; Van Dam *et al.* 2012). While the wide variety of initiatives that characterize these alternative networks is beginning to be better documented in the literature, joint purchasing groups have clearly received most of the attention. Initially, these groups predominantly brought consumers together to buy from one or a handful of producers in a circumscribed geographical area. The groups operate according to a democratic self-managed model and rely almost exclusively on voluntary resources. At their inception, actual member participation (contact with producers, preparation of packages, organization of distribution) is expected and purely consumerist attitudes are discouraged (Coen 2010).

The effective involvement of members in the group's activity is a necessity at first. Indeed, even though the short food supply chain allows the group to avoid the cost of intermediation, this necessarily means that it must shoulder coordination costs (between supply and demand) and forgo economies of scale enabled by supply centres and supermarket distribution channels. Unless they set very high prices, the model is not naturally "profitable" for producers; recourse to member volunteerism allows them, at least initially, to set reasonable prices.

Participation is also an important factor in enabling citizens to ensure the quality of the products they buy. Trust builds through the geographic proximity of consumers and producers (Deverre and Lamine 2010; Holzemer *et al.* 2015) as well as due to the absence of intermediaries with purely commercial motivations, who are potential sources of sanitary negligence. This is a key argument because, according to Thys (2013), most consumer members of these initiatives acknowledge that personal concerns about health and the risks involved in consuming industrial food products informed their commitment to the group. Thys notes that these members are often unaware – at least when they first join the group – of the difficulties related to local organic agricultural production, and they are not always concerned about environmental matters. The element of social consciousness, however – this solidarity with small producers – is often a primary driver, especially in the case of those who initiate such projects.

Authors who study the discourse of active participants in these groups emphasize that motivations and their intensity develop and change over time. It appears that participants' reasoning is enriched and becomes multidimensional over the course of discussions with other group members. Initial discourses, focused on very "individualistic" issues pertaining to the risks associated with consuming agribusiness products, gradually evolve into more "altruistic" discourses that take into account the societal repercussions of the act of buying (Marsden and Smith 2005; Seyfang 2006; Plateau 2013). We can see a translation of this gradual evolution of motivations in the activities carried out by the groups. Structures such as simple joint purchasing groups may develop into more complex systems where consumers come into regular contact with producers (Lamine 2008) and, little by little, conceive of ways to support the producers, such as prepayment systems and order regularity. In doing this, they share the risks of production and provide the farmer with a predictable income (Coen 2010). It is not uncommon to see these groups encourage the establishment or the conversion of certain agricultural facilities by helping secure access to land or by supporting the development of training courses in organic market gardening. Overall, beyond the discursive developments, we thus observe learning phenomena generated by participation in these initiatives – be it in terms of agricultural, culinary or democratic practices – as a source of empowerment for these new "food citizens" (Domaneschi 2012; Holzemer *et al.* 2015).

Finally, when these groups seek to establish themselves durably – in particular, due to their growth or because the issues they wish to address are expanding – they use the legal forms of the non-profit association and the cooperative (the latter of which allows them to have a broader financial base (Coen 2010)). It is also the institutionalization of these groups that allows them to fit into larger structures, as with the combination of joint purchasing groups and producer cooperatives within multi-actor short food supply chains (Messmer 2013) or local food hubs, which are veritable logistics centres (Cleveland *et al.* 2014).

Conclusion

Most economists consider capitalist ownership as the universal archetype for organizations, while other forms of ownership are viewed as throwbacks to archaic stages of development, destined to disappear at the pace of global economic growth. Given the persistence of cooperatives and associations within our economies, however, we must question this belief. Moreover, these organizational forms could play a major role in the necessary social and ecological transition. Indeed, their different institutional characteristics make them particularly well-suited to provide frameworks for local collective initiatives as well as to help in overcoming the free rider problem. The cases of the energy and agri-food sectors show that citizens' initiatives can spearhead the implementation of alternative logics of production and consumption despite the considerable inertial forces that characterize the current models. Social economy organizations provide these initiatives with legal frameworks and management tools that can help them transcend their still marginal position in our societies' institutional and economic landscapes.

The advantages presented by social economy organizations can only be put to good use if we conceive of the social and ecological transition towards a post-growth society in polycentric terms. While the social and environmental contexts in which public management processes take place are becoming increasingly complex and uncertain, we consider that a polycentric regime is capable of providing a flexible and adaptive governance framework for the transition. As such, it is incumbent on public policy-makers to create favourable conditions for collective action by local actors – in other words, to minimize the cost of their self-organization. They must also ensure the coordination of the system by guaranteeing that the rules common to all initiatives are respected.

These considerations suggest different avenues for future research. First, despite the growing popularity of the concept of polycentric governance, its potential for comprehending complex socio-economic systems (and the problems of collective action in particular) is still largely in need of scholarly attention. Second, we must conduct more in-depth research into the processes of citizen-based self-organization, especially in regard to the phenomena of initiative hybridization, the organizational forms suited to these initiatives, and the effects of these forms on the behaviour of the individuals who use them. The present chapter has hopefully shown the potential of social economy organizations in this respect, but the roles of these organizations in the transition's polycentric governance systems remain largely unexplored.

This discussion also questions the theoretical foundations of conventional economics from several points of view. First, the polycentric view of collective action calls for individuals to be considered not only as passive consumers or simple beneficiaries of social policies, but also as "citizens" capable of taking charge of their common fate and thus becoming "co-producers" of public affairs. Second, the polycentric approach to governance leads to recognition of the diversity and complexity of economic actors and their modes of coordination. Thus, not all firms pursue the maximization of profits, not all individuals are selfish, and there clearly exist other structures of coordination than the market and the state.

Notes

1 While we refer to "the transition" in the singular, this term must not obscure the fact that there are in reality *several* transitions, as necessary changes in very different domains will probably follow disparate trajectories.
2 Here we use the term "social economy" in the sense of a collection of private organizations that share in the pursuit of a social goal, the exercise of economic democracy in their governing bodies, and the allocation of benefits according to a non-capitalist mode. These organizations mostly take the form of associations and cooperatives. The preferred term in France is "*économie sociale et solidaire*" [social and solidarity economy].
3 A Pigovian tax enables the collective negative externalities created by the production or the use of a product to be incorporated into the real cost of said product. It is often described as an application of the "polluter pays" principle.

References

Aligica, P.D. and Tarko, V. (2012). Polycentricity: From Polanyi to Ostrom, and Beyond. *Governance*, 25: 237–262. doi:10.1111/j.1468-0491.2011.01550.x

Andersson, K.P. and Ostrom, E. (2008). Analyzing Decentralized Resource Regimes from a Polycentric Perspective. *Policy Sciences*, 41: 71–93. doi:www.springerlink.com/link.asp?id=102982.

Anheier, H.K. and Ben-Ner, A. (2002). *The Study of the Nonprofit Enterprise*. New York: Kluwer.

Bauwens, T. (2015). Propriété coopérative et acceptabilité sociale de l'éolien terrestre. *Reflets et Perspectives de la Vie Economique*, LIV: 59–70.

Bauwens, T. (2016). Explaining the Diversity of Motivations behind Community Renewable Energy. *Energy Policy*, 93: 278–290. doi:10.1016/j.enpol.2016.03.017.

Bauwens, T. and Eyre, N. (2017). Exploring the Links between Community-Based Governance and Sustainable Energy Use: Quantitative Evidence from Flanders. *Ecological Economics*, 137: 163–172. doi:10.1016/j.ecolecon.2017.03.006.

Bauwens, T., Gotchev, B. and Holstenkamp, L. (2016). What Drives the Development of Community Energy in Europe? The Case of Wind Power Cooperatives. *Energy Research and Social Sciences*, 13: 136–147. doi:10.1016/j.erss.2015.12.016.

Becchetti, L., Castriota, S. and Tortia, E. (2013). Productivity, Wages and Intrinsic Motivations. *Small Business Economics*, 41: 379–399. doi:10.1007/s11187-012-9431-2.

Benz, M. (2005). Not for the Profit, but for the Satisfaction? Evidence on Worker Well-Being in Non-Profit Firms. *Kyklos*, 58: 155–176. doi:10.1111/j.0023-5962.2005.00283.x.

Borzaga, C. and Tortia, E. (2006). Worker Motivations, Job Satisfaction, and Loyalty in Public and Nonprofit Social Services. *Nonprofit and Voluntary Sector Quarterly*, 35: 225–248. doi:10.1177/0899764006287207.

Cleveland, D.A., Müller, N.M., Tranovich, A.C., Mazaroli, D.N. and Hinson, K. (2014). Local Food Hubs for Alternative Food Systems: A Case Study from Santa Barbara County, California. *Journal of Rural Studies*, 35: 26–36. doi:10.1016/j.jrurstud.2014.03.008.

Coen, J.M. (2010). Alimentations et circuits courts, Initiatives citoyennes, l'économie sociale de demain. *Les dossiers de l'économie sociale*, SAW-B: 26–77.

Defourny, J. and Develtere, P. (2000). The Social Economy: The Worldwide Making of a Third Sector. In J. Defourny, P. Develtere and B. Fonteneau (eds), *Social Economy in North and South*. HIVA/Centre d'Économie Sociale-ULg, Liège/Leuven, pp. 17–47.

Deverre, C. and Lamine, C. (2010). Les systèmes agroalimentaires alternatifs. Une revue de travaux anglophones en sciences sociales. *Économie rurale*, 317: 57–73.

DiMaggio, P.J. and Powell, W.W. (1983). The Iron Cage Revisited: Institutional Isomorphism and Collective Rationality in Organizational Fields. *American Sociological Review*, 48: 147–160. doi:10.2307/2095101.

Domaneschi, L. (2012). Food Social Practices: Theory of Practice and the New Battlefield of Food Quality. *Journal of Consumer Culture*, 12: 306–322. doi:10.1177/1469540512456919.

Downs, A. (1957). An Economic Theory of Political Action in a Democracy. *Journal of Political Economy*, 65: 135–150.

Frey, B. (1997). *Not Just for the Money: An Economic Theory of Personal Motivation*. Cheltenham: Edward Elgar.

Friedman, M. (1970). The Social Responsibility of Business is to Increase its Profits. *New York Times Magazine*.

Granovetter, M.S. (1973). The Strength of Weak Ties. *American Journal of Sociology*, 78: 1360–1380. doi:10.2307/2776392.

Hansmann, H. (1980). The Role of Non-Profit Enterprise. *Yale Law Journal*, 89: 835–901.

Hansmann, H. (1996). *The Ownership of Enterprise*. Cambridge, MA: The Belknap Press of Harvard University Press.

Holzemer, L., Marcq, P., Plateau, L., Mertens, S. and Maréchal, K. (2015). Circuits courts alimentaires en Wallonie: hybridation des pratiques des mangeurs et des modes d'organisation. *Working paper projet CADACC*, présenté au 2ème congrès du développement durable, Louvain-la-Neuve ULB-ULg.

Huybrechts, B. and Mertens, S. (2014). The Relevance of the Cooperative Model in the Field of Renewable Energy. *Annals of Public and Cooperative Economics*, 85: 193–212. doi:10.1111/apce.12038.

Kemp, R., Schot, J. and Hoogma, R. (1998). Regime Shifts to Sustainability through Processes of Niche Formation: The Approach of Strategic Niche Management. *Technology Analysis & Strategic Management*, 10: 175–198. doi:10.1080/09537329808524310.

Lamine, C. (2008). *Les amaps, un nouveau pacte entre producteurs et consommateurs?* Gap: Éditions Yves Michel.

Laskey, A. and Syler, B. (2013). The Ultimate Challenge: Getting Consumers Engaged in Energy Efficency. In F.P. Sioshansi (ed.), *Energy Efficiency: Towards the End of Demand Growth*. Oxford: Academic Press, pp. 591–612.

Maréchal, K. (2010). Not Irrational but Habitual: The Importance of "Behavioural Lock-In" in Energy Consumption. *Ecological Economics*, 69: 1104–1114. doi:10.1016/j.ecolecon.2009.12.004.

Marsden, T. and Smith, E. (2005). Ecological Entrepreneurship: Sustainable Development in Local Communities through Quality Food Production and Local Branding. *Geoforum*, 36: 440–451. doi:10.1016/j.geoforum.2004.07.008.

Marshall, G. (2005). *Economics for Collaborative Environmental Management: Renegotiating the Commons*. London: Earthscan.

Mertens, S. (2010). De l'initiative citoyenne à l'entreprise d'économie sociale. In *Initiatives Citoyennes, L'économie Sociale de Demain?* Etude SAW-B, pp. 12–24.

Messmer, J.G. (2013). Les circuits courts multi-acteurs : émergence d'organisations innovantes dans les filières courtes alimentaires. *Rapport INRA-MaR/S*.

Milgrom, P. and Roberts, J. (1992). *Economics, Organization and Management*. Englewood Cliffs: Prentice Hall International.

Olson, M. (1965). *The Logic of Collective Action: Public Goods and the Theory of Groups*. Cambridge, MA: Harvard University Press.

Ostrom, E. (1990). *Governing the Commons: The Evolution of Institutions for Collective Action, Political Economy of Institutions and Decisions*. Cambridge: Cambridge University Press.

Ostrom, E. (2010). Polycentric Systems for Coping with Collective Action and Global Environmental Change. *Global Environmental Change*, 20: 550–557. doi:10.1016/j.gloenvcha.2010.07.004.

Ostrom, V., Tiebout, C.M. and Warren, R. (1961). The Organization of Government in Metropolitan Areas: A Theoretical Inquiry. *American Political Sciences Review*, 55: 831–842. doi:10.2307/1952530.

Plateau, L. (2013). Groupes d'achat solidaire de l'agriculture paysanne: un exemple d'encastrement de l'économie dans la société. De la délibération pour une économie solidaire fertile. *Mémoire de fin d'études*, ULB.

Rose-Ackerman, S. (1996). Altruism, Nonprofits, and Economic Theory. *Journal of Economic Litterature*, 34: 701–728.

Samuelson, P.A. (1954). The Pure Theory of Public Expenditure. *The Review of Economics and Statistics*, 36: 387–389. doi:10.2307/1925895.

Santos, F. (2012). A Positive Theory of Social Entrepreneurship. *Journal of Business Ethics*, 111: 335–351. doi:10.1007/s10551-012-1413-4.

Seyfang, G. (2006). Ecological Citizenship and Sustainable Consumption: Examining Local Organic Food Networks. *Journal of Rural Studies*, 22: 383–395. doi:10.1016/j.jrurstud.2006.01.003.

Spear, R. (2000). The Co-operative Advantage. *Annals of Public and Cooperative Economics*, 71: 507–523. doi:10.1111/1467-8292.00151.

Steinberg, R. (2006). Economic Theories of Nonprofit Organisations. In *The Nonprofit Sector: A Research Handbook*. New Haven: Yale University Press, pp. 117–139.

Thys, S. (2013). De consommateurs à citoyens. Avec quelle force les consom'acteurs participent-ils à la Transition? Le cas du Commerce équitable et des GAC. 4th EMES International Research Conference on Social Enterprise: "If Not For Profit, For What? And How?", Liège.

Tyler, T.R. and Blader, S.L. (2001). Identity and Cooperative Behavior in Groups. *Group Process and Intergroup Relations*, 4: 207–226. doi:10.1177/1368430201004003003.

Van Dam, D., Streith, M., Nizet, J. and Stassart, P. (2012). *La gouvernance des groupements d'achat alimentaires et ses paradoxes*. Dijon: Educagri.

Weisbrod, B.A. (1975). Toward a Theory of the Voluntary Nonprofit Sector in a Three-Sector Economy. In E.S. Phelps (ed.), *Altruism, Morality, and Economic Theory*. New York: Russell Sage Foundation, pp. 171–196.

5 Circular economy in a territorial context

The case of biowaste management in Brussels

Stephan Kampelmann

The term "circular economy" has been coined in opposition to the idea of linear flows, i.e. movements of materials or energy that begin with the extraction of a resource and end with the creation of waste. Over the last decade, circular economy has moved from a pioneering ambition into the limelight of corporate and public policy: numerous multinationals (including Philips, Unilever, Renault, Nike, Cisco and Google) now present themselves as ardent promoters of this novel avenue of doing business. Various European metropoles (Paris, Rotterdam, Amsterdam, Brussels, etc.) have launched programmes and initiatives to render their economies more circular. The European Commission also aims to foster this transition and presented an ambitious Circular Economy Package for the European Union. Ever more zealous, China presents itself as the spearhead of this movement: virtually all Chinese development plans written in recent years refer to circular economy as an overarching guiding principle. Consultancies and private foundations have not been at rest either. Organizations such as the UK-based Ellen MacArthur Foundation or the New Economics Foundation have churned out an abundant literature on the merits of circular business models. Finally, academia has started to explore the notion of circular economy, for instance by relating it to earlier strands of research such as Industrial Ecology.

The objective of this chapter is not to analyse the vast, often politicized and extremely polymorphic discourse on circular economy. Instead, we employ the notion of circularization as an ideal-type – never attainable, but under certain conditions desirable – that could serve as a signpost for social-ecological transitions. But while many are those who agree that the circularization of the economy appears to be a sensible strategy for achieving biophysical resource sustainability, our contribution points out that there are alternative paths that can lead us there. Crucially, these alternatives differ with respect to their economic, social and environmental consequences. More specifically, we compare two contrasting trajectories: one of a "third industrial revolution" that prolongs the logic of economic growth based on capital accumulation and quantitative expansion; and a trajectory of "post-growth" that would rely on a new polycentric organization of work and a qualitative, less capital-intensive form of development.

On a theoretical level, our analysis builds on the theory of social-ecological systems, an interdisciplinary approach that blends knowledge on biophysical (ecosystems, material flows, natural cycles, etc.) and anthropic (institutions, rules, actors, etc.) phenomena. Taken together, these elements form the complex systems in which economic activity evolves. This theoretical framework allows us to account for the embeddedness of economic activities in both biophysical and socio-political realities.

Empirically, we illustrate alternative pathways towards circularization for the case of organic matter in the city-region of Brussels. The social-ecological system of Brussels is particularly interesting: competing initiatives that could scale up into scenarios of a "third industrial revolution" or "post-growth" currently co-exist in this city.

Finally, the fourth section compares these two potential social-ecological trajectories towards more circularity of organic flows with respect to their economic, social and environmental implications. Given that the regional government repeatedly expressed its political will to render its economy more circular (a Regional Programme for Circular Economy has been adopted in March 2016), our analysis could inform the public choice among available options for the case of biowaste management.

Theoretical framework

Circularization of economic flows

The use of the term "circular economy" has been applied to an array of heterogeneous ideas at different scales such as waste reduction, the restoration of natural resources, the generation of renewable energies, the creation of entrepreneurial opportunities, a new industrial revolution, the relaunch of economic growth in Europe and the sustainability of growth in emerging countries (Lyle 1985; Stahel 2010; McDonough and Braungart 2002; Ellen MacArthur Foundation and Granta Design 2015). The meaning of the term in non-scientific language has been shaped by consultants, private foundations, multinational corporations and governments at different levels. The fuzzy and polysemic character of "circular economy" might explain why the term has yet to make significant inroads into the scientific literature, especially in economics.

Since it is therefore difficult to extract a robust and clear definition from the use of "circular economy" in public discourse, we propose a definition in form of two mutually exclusive Weberian ideal-types:

* *Linear flows.* These are material or energy flows that start with the extraction of a resource, go through a phase of transformation and consumption and end up as waste. Since the second half of the nineteenth century, all economic activities resemble this ideal-type in that they rely on the extraction of raw materials and generate waste in variable but always positive quantities (Georgescu-Roegen 1987; McNeill 2001).

- *Circular flows*. These flows have neither clear beginning nor end: when a certain process ejects a substance, the latter is then consumed as useful input by another process. The flows in the natural cycles described by scientific ecology (the cycles of water, nitrogen, carbon, etc.) resemble this ideal-type.

According to this definition, we can label a flow as being "circular" if it is sufficiently similar to natural cycles that fulfil the conditions of: (1) not producing any waste; and (2) moving in perfectly closed loops. Similarly, a "circular economy" can be defined as an economic system whose biophysical functioning resembles an ecosystem, i.e. "an ensemble of all the vegetal, animal and microbial populations grouped together in a specific milieu" that is integrated in its environment in a "functioning ecological system" (Duvigneaud 1974). Like an ecosystem, circular economy is thus characterized by a very peculiar type of metabolism in which vital processes terminate with a "separation" instead of waste creation; this "separation" then gives rise to a "consumption" at the start of another vital process. The more an economic system is similar to a waste-free, closed-loop ecosystem, the more it becomes "circular" (see Kampelmann and De Muynck, forthcoming).

The analogy between economic systems and ecosystem is one of the hallmarks of Industrial Ecology, a field that studies technological systems in which the waste streams of one industrial operator become the inputs of other operators (Gallopoulos 2006). The emblematic showcase of Industrial Ecology is the industrial park in the Danish city of Kalundborg. It should, however, be noted that "ecological" industrial systems such as the one in Kalundborg hardly ever produce fully closed loops that can be likened to a natural ecosystem; rather than returning a substance to the process that has produced it in the first place, systems like Kalundborg only reuse a given substance before it inevitably turns to waste at a later stage. As a consequence, the systems theorized by Industrial Ecology tend to *defer* the production of waste, but fall short of *eliminating* waste altogether (Arnsperger and Bourg 2016).

At first sight, it appears highly attractive to reconfigure economic systems so that they mimic natural ecosystems. But upon reflection it can be argued that the circularization of material flows alone is not a sufficient criterion to evaluate the desirability of alternative development trajectories. In some cases, the circulation of a substance can have negative environmental effects, for example due to a rise in energy consumption. If material loops are too extensive and the transformation processes they require too energy-intensive – as has been documented for the circulation of certain biopolymers – the corollary negative environmental impacts might outweigh the benefits of material circularity. In other cases, the circularization of material flows can spark social conflicts, for instance when agricultural land is dedicated to the production of biofuels instead of the cultivation of food. Finally, a circularization initiative can also have negative economic consequences, for instance if it replaces labour-intensive production by automated procedures. To be sure, the circularization of flows is only economically sustainable if the costs of raw materials are higher than the costs of maintaining the secondary materials in circulation.

This means that circularization initiatives are not an end in themselves, but should rather be judged by their economic, social and environmental consequences. Needless to say that this requires extremely complex evaluations that risk running into the thorny trade-offs that have been documented by the literature on multidimensional indicators (Bruno *et al.* 2016). The Ellen MacArthur Foundation (2015) proposes to address this multidimensionality by adding "complementary indicators" regarding water use, energy consumption or GHG emissions to its Material Circularity Indicator. But the literature on circular economy still fails to provide clear indications how to deal with trade-offs between these different indicators: should we consider a company that uses more raw materials but less energy as less "circular" than another company that uses less materials and more energy?

In this chapter, we propose to evaluate different circularization strategies with the help of system analysis. Drawing on studies from both the natural and social sciences, our approach underlines the close links between biophysical and anthropogenic systems that are captured by the theory of "social-ecological systems" (Dietz *et al.* 2003; Holling 2006) or "socioecological regimes" (Fischer-Kowalski and Haberl 2007). This allows us to envisage circular economy in a wider field of complex interactions and to think of their multidimensional consequences in terms of "socioecological trajectory" (Barles 2015), i.e. a narrative of a multidimensional co-evolution.

Terminology and analysis of social-ecological systems

Due to the assembly of different sub-systems and a large number of variables in constant interaction, social-ecological systems are extremely complex research objects. But this complexity should not be mistaken for unintelligible chaos; indeed, several academic traditions have successfully explored and analysed complex systems. While theological worldviews have long crowded out scientific forms of system analysis, they have reappeared in Western philosophy in the wake of the Enlightenment. But it was only in the 1970s that system analysis started to revolutionize the understanding of complex biotopes such as forests or oceans by framing them as intelligible ecosystems. Almost simultaneously, a group of MIT scientists applied system analysis to the evolution of an array of biophysical and economic variables to estimate the "limits to growth" beyond which global production systems would become unstable. Historically and intellectually rooted in engineering science, today system analysis is a full-fledged academic discipline. In parallel, other disciplines have developed specific theories on monetary, solar, scholar or legal systems.

Among the most relevant theories for our purposes comes from the interdisciplinary literature concerned with the analysis of social-ecological systems and their metabolism (Fischer-Kowalski and Haberl 2007). While most authors study social-ecological systems at the macroscopic scale, a rapidly expanding literature looks at territorial metabolism, and in particular at the metabolism of urban agglomerations (Barles 2010; Kampelmann and De Muynck forthcoming).

It is probably worthwhile noting that Belgium, and in particular the Brussels School under the influence of Paul Duvigneaud, was in the 1970s the theatre of a first wave of progress in the understanding of social-ecological systems. Indeed, the book *L'écosystème Belgique* [*Ecosystem Belgium*] by Billen *et al.* (1983) is a remarkable early attempt at applying methods of scientific ecology to the analysis of the industrial system of Belgium. Its subtitle, "A study in industrial ecology", is a hint that the book already anticipated the distinction between linear and circular industrial systems. It is thus unfortunate that the pioneering contributions by Duvigneaud's School have been pushed to the margin of the Belgian academic landscape; it is only very recently that holistic analyses such as the "Ecosystem Belgium" (Billen *et al.* 1983) and "Ecosystem Brussels" (Duvigneaud and Denayer-De Smet 1975) have reappeared in research programmes in this country.

In terms of methods, the system analysis of Duvigneaud and his colleagues was mostly based on elaborate flow diagrams. This echoed the kind of representations used in scientific ecology to describe phenomena like the nitrogen or the carbon cycle. Unsurprisingly, the complexity of a social-ecological object such as the Belgian industrial system was framed by Billen and his co-authors in analogy to Duvigneaud's seminal representation of a forest, in which the interconnections of numerous cycles give rise to an overarching ecosystem. By contrast, the more recent perspective developed by social scientists such as Elinor Ostrom and others put the emphasis on the roles of actors and their interactions, as well as the rules and institutions that govern social-ecological systems (Ostrom 2007, 2008). Our intention in this chapter is to work towards combining these two traditions by accounting not only for the material cycles that were the focus of Duvigneaud's School, but also the institutional factors emphasized by Ostrom's approach.

The first step in system analysis boils down to a characterization of the system one wants to study. In the case of a social-ecological system, such a characterization encompasses elements of heterogeneous nature that we propose to group into three distinct sets. A first set of elements refers to *actions* and includes the actors of the systems and the interactions between these actors. A second set is concerned with the *biophysical* elements and characterizes the spaces of the system (e.g. a valley, a neighbourhood, a centre, a periphery, etc.), its artefacts (a factory, different types of products) and the material and energy flows passing through the system. Finally, a third set refers to *framing* elements such as the domain of the system, its rules and its scale.

These generic elements of a social-ecological system thus combine the perspectives of Paul Duvigneaud and Elinor Ostrom: the material flows as well as the scale and spaces that organize these flows are directly borrowed from the analysis of ecosystems as described by the Ecological Synthesis (Duvigneaud 1974); the domain of the system, its actors and their interactions plus the rules that govern the system are inspired by the Institutional Analysis and Development Framework by Ostrom (2010).

The management system of organic matter in Brussels

In this section we sketch the current configuration of the social-ecological system that governs the flows of organic matter in Brussels; we also examine which of these flows can be likened to the ideal-types of linear and circular flows defined above.

Before we describe the specificities of the case of Brussels, it should be noted that urban organic matter is an issue of high relevance in both economic and ecologic terms. This is primarily due to the large quantities that they represent: around 40 per cent of solid municipal waste in Europe. But reforming urban biowaste management is also salient because of the stubbornly low rate of selective collection; according to the European Compost Network, only 30 per cent of biowaste is currently collected and treated separately from other solid municipal waste. Reducing the amount of organic matter sent to landfills could pay off, especially if it is combined with the production of energy and other valuable substances from biowaste. For the United Kingdom, the Ellen MacArthur Foundation estimates these benefits at $1.1 billion and 2 GWh of electricity per year (Ellen MacArthur and Granta Design Foundation 2015). At the global scale, Steffen *et al.* (2015) argue that the current overconsumption of nitrogen and phosphorus oversteps planetary limits, as 118 million kilos of phosphorus appear to be lost every year (Jonckhoff and Van der Kooij 2015). Closing the cycles of nitrogen and phosphorus, two mineral substances that are essential for agriculture and contained in large quantities in urban biowaste, emerges thus as a priority to avoid the planetary instabilities flagged by Steffen *et al.* (2015). What is more, the circularization of organic matter passing through urban agglomerations appears to be imperative in the fight against the erosion of arable land in Europe and elsewhere (Servigne 2014).

Domain

In this chapter we employ the term "domain" to refer to the sum of functions that are organized by the system. In essence, the domain therefore defines functional boundaries. The domain of the current system that governs the flows of organic matter in Brussels includes not only organic residues and human/animal excrements, but also flows of drinking water and black water. The reason for this is that a considerable portion of organic matter is transported out of the cities through the sewage system, which is therefore inextricably intertwined with the system of organic matter. In addition to the agricultural industry, peri-urban and even urban agriculture appears to play an increasing role in the current system, notably due to a growing demand for local food and urban horticulture. Finally, the domain also encompasses the indigenous biological production and the energy supply of the city-region of Brussels – two functions that were governed by completely separate systems until the 1980s.

Scale

The scale of the system is defined by the size of its stocks – the system in Brussels organizes the flows of 1,120,000 inhabitants, 350,000 commuters and at least as many pets – and of its incoming and outgoing flows. The geographic scale of the system reflects the dispersion of these flows in space. Today, most of the outgoing flows are managed by a series of industrial facilities at the periphery of the metropolis. While the scale of some of the flows is continental or even global (notably the incoming foodstuffs), others are mostly national (drinking water from Wallonia, biowaste treatment in Flanders), and most of them are regional (incineration, sewage treatment and composting).

Actors

The nineteen municipalities of the Brussels-Capital Region enjoy limited autonomy in the area of waste management. Among other tasks, they are in charge of cleaning municipal roads, run municipal waste collection centres and manage green waste from municipal parks and street trees. Since the Region of Brussels was created 1989 as a third federated Belgian region next to Wallonia and Flanders, the regional government and its agencies are the principal political actor of the system. The ministry in charge of waste management is currently delegated to the Secretary of State Fadila Lanaan. Among other elements, the regional government can influence the rules that govern the system, for example the laws on mandatory waste sorting or through public procurement in the area of waste collection and waste treatment. It uses the taxes it collects to fund the key actors of the system as well as a series of infrastructures that are essential to the current form of biowaste management in Brussels.

The current system is characterized by a large number of public operators: in addition to the operators in charge of the transportation, distribution and evacuation of water (in Brussels these functions are distributed among four different public agencies), we need to mention the principal public operator for the collection and sorting of waste, the Agence Bruxelles Propreté (ABP). While the different public operators are frequently criticized for their organization in silos, there are also more transversal institutions such as the Brussels Environment Agency under the responsibility of the Ministry of Environment. Recent initiatives such as the Employment Environment Alliance, the Brussels Waste Network or the Regional Programme for Circular Economy also aim for better coordination between the different elements of the system.

A substantial part of the system's management is currently delegated to a group of private actors, mostly in the form of public–private partnerships (PPPs): the multinational companies Veolia, Suez and Indaver, for instance, play key roles in the system.

As for the production of biowaste, the principal actors are private households, companies in the food sector and other institutions offering catering services (schools, administrations, large offices with canteens, prisons, etc.). Other biodegradable waste stems from parks and gardens and is produced by municipal and regional services, gardening and landscape companies and private owners of gardens.

It is remarkable that a growing number of households act not only as producers of biowaste, but also engage in its treatment through composting. According to a survey by Brussels Environment from 2012, 17 per cent of citizens engage in some form of composting (a figure that is seven percentage points higher compared to 2000). Collective composting is supported by different local environmental NGOs (Worms asbl, Le Début des Haricots asbl, the Urban Ecology Centre asbl, etc.), as well as by local and regional administrations. This support often takes the form of training programmes in which more than 400 "master composters" have been trained in the art of producing high-quality compost.

Interactions/flows

The interactions between the regional government, the public utilities and the PPPs give rise to substantial financial flows. In addition to the 48 million euro in revenues it collects from private households, ABP receives an annual dotation of 140 million euro; according the organization's activity report, annual expenditures in 2013 exceeded 190 million euro, of which 30–40 per cent can be attributed to the management of biowaste. The collection of sewage also amounts to a sizable budget. For example, the SBGE, the public utility in charge of the network of sewers and collectors, reports annual expenses of more than 70.6 million euro for 2013.

One of the consequences of PPPs in the waste sector is the complexity of the financial and legal relationships between the different actors that they bring together. The waste incinerator located in Neder-Over-Heembeek is operated by a private company called Bruxelles-Energie sprl, 60 per cent owned by the ABP and 40 per cent by the multinational Suez Environnement; the composting facility in the municipality of Forest is run by the private company Bruxelles-Compost sa (60 per cent ABP, 40 per cent Indaver – a multinational with an annual turnover of 203 million euro in Belgium); the water treatment plan "North" is operated by Acquiris, a subsidiary of Veolia Water, in exchange of an annual sum of 41 million euro in 2013–2014. The anaerobic digestion plant in Ypres (Flanders) is controlled by IVVO cvba, a PPP between several local Flemish authorities and the aforementioned Indaver. While we are not able to quantify the exact size of all financial flows in these sprawling partnerships, we estimate them to exceed several hundred euro per year per inhabitant. This reflects of course the relatively large volumes of waste that are put through the system every year, but also contrasts starkly with the *profitable* system which prevailed in the first half of the nineteenth century (see Kohlbrenner 2014).

Moreover, despite the hefty sums that the current system pays to private corporations, the relationships within the PPPs are often tense and frequently spark legal conflicts. A memorable case of such a conflict was the stand-still of one of

Brussels' two sewage plants in December 2009, an incident that followed a rift between Veolia and its public partners. Shortly after the incident with serious environmental fallout for the Senne and other connected water streams, several Flemish public authorities situated downstream filed legal complaints, some of which are still ongoing. Moreover, a case currently heard by a Brussels Court opposes the public agency SBGE and Veolia for what the French company claims to be an unsettled bill of 5.5 million euro before taxes.

The system also gives rise to sums flowing in the opposite direction, i.e. which are generated by the treatment of biowaste. This is chiefly the case for the production of energy by the incinerator, an activity that is estimated to cover circa 10 per cent of Brussels' electrical consumption. This being said, the contribution of organic matter (30–50 per cent of the facility's inputs) to the energy production is small or even negative due to its high water content (around 80 per cent). Other inverted financial flows include the commercialization of "technosable", a product extracted from the sewage plant, and the sale of compost by the facilities in Forest (in the Brussels-Capital Region) and Grimbergen (in Flanders).

The sale of approximately 9,200 t/y of compost is the only outflow of significant size that is given back to agriculture. It is absorbed by a few farmers from the Walloon Brabant buying it at around 5 euro/t (Brussels Environment 2015). While it is true that this flow transports mineral nutrients from the city to regional agriculture, it cannot be likened to a circular flow. This is because Bruxelles-Compost produces the compost using around 17,000 t/y of green waste collected from the indigenous vegetation of the capital (parks, gardens, street trees, etc.)[1] – it therefore does not stem from the importation of food from regional agriculture. This is also the reason why the nitrogen and phosphate content of this compost is so low that it can hardly be considered as an effective mineral or biological fertilizer. The residues of plastic bags that are present in the compost also diminish its commercial value. All other organic flows are linear and are not reinjected into *extra-muros* agriculture, notably the circa 144,000 t/y of biowaste collected from households (123 kg/hab/y) that are incinerated every year (Brussels Environment 2015).

One way of directing organic matter back to agriculture could take the form of up-scaling the currently minuscule quantities that are sent to a biogas plant in Ypres. Biomethanization is a bio-industrial procedure whose main objective is to generate energy: the methane produced by the plant in Ypres is converted into electricity, albeit in a process whose efficiency is limited to 30 per cent. The efficiency is much higher when the gas is directly used as thermal energy (heating, combustion engines). At the end of the anaerobic digestion, it is equally possible to mix the digestate with an additional dose of carbon-rich material and oxygen so as to obtain compost that can be sold to farmers – much like the urban manure that cities produced in substantial quantities during the nineteenth century (Barles 2015). This being said, the political actors of the Brussels region do not have any control over the plant in Ypres, which is situated 130 kilometres away from the metropolis. On any account, the Ypres plant's capacity is limited at

25,000 t/y and could therefore only treat a fraction of the 144,000 t that are collected each year in Brussels. Another serious limitation for the systemic use of compost from anaerobic digestion is its potential contamination with plastic residues, heavy metals (lead, cadmium) and organic pollutants (PAHs).

Through the intervention of 17 per cent of the population of Brussels who compost their biowaste, a share of the indigenous biomass is mixed with nitrogen-rich kitchen waste. The government invests in this activity through small grants and subsidies provided by the Ministry of Environment in the context of awareness-raising policies directed at community composts. The latter are considered as means to waste prevention rather than waste treatment (Dennemont 2012). The NGO Worms has compiled a list of around hundred community compost stations that are estimated to treat between 300 and 520 t/y of biowaste. In all cases that we are aware of, the compost produced by community composts is reinjected into the regional ecosystem. Like the mineral-rich urban manure of the nineteenth century, decentralized composting benefits constantly from external inputs imported from agriculture. By retaining the nutrients in the city, it thereby contributes to the concentration of minerals in the urban centres, which effectively behave like "nitrogen sinks".

Spaces/artefacts

The spaces and artefacts of the current system reflect two alternative tendencies that co-exist at present. The first boils down to a centralized treatment with the help of industrial facilities. Due to the acoustic, olfactive and aesthetic nuisances that they typically engender, these facilities have been located at the fringe of the urban core: a sorting plant, a composting plant, the incinerator, two sewage plants, etc. These installations are connected through extensive road, water and energy networks of regional proportions. The second and quite different tendency is the decentralized treatment through a series of spaces and artefacts that are situated within the city, like the individual or collective compost stations.

The most visible and recognizable artefact of the current system is surely the almost iconic plastic bag that ABP employs for the collection of solid municipal waste from households. Depending on its content, this bag comes in a palette of colours (white, blue, yellow, green, orange). Being made of non-recycled polymers, the hundreds of thousands of plastic bags used to collect waste in Brussels constitute in themselves a rather massive form of waste.

Rules

The different European Directives concerning the treatment of black water and biowaste have been highly influential for the development of the current system. The Framework Directive N°2008/98/CE, for instance, fixes EU-wide objectives for the proportion of waste that should be collected and treated separately from the rest of solid municipal waste. An equally influential but much more fuzzy set of rules are those that define the notions of ecology and sustainable development in the context of waste management. A recurrent indicator is the production of energy from "renewable" sources. The government of Brussels has attributed so-called Green Certificates to the incinerator operated by ABP/Suez, a decision that politicians justified by the production of "renewable energy" through the combustion of garbage (based on the rather absurd proposition that waste is a "renewable resource"). Since renewable energy is currently considered a priority over other rules, it tilts the system of biowaste management towards technologies that generate energy, such as incineration or anaerobic digestion. On any account, this rule appears to override other desirable outcomes such as the return of nutrients to agriculture.

Another set of influential rules is related to the financial and legal framework that underpins the numerous PPPs. These rules define the form and content of public procurement processes leading up to these partnerships, including how costs and financial risks are split among the partners. Even if only regional authorities and private companies enter these public procurement processes, an important part of these rules are created by political instances at higher scales, especially the European Commission.

The interdependence between domain, spaces and rules appears clearly in the current configuration of the system. Contrary to the situation in more progressive cities like Seattle or many urban agglomerations in Italy, sorting of biowaste is not mandatory in Brussels. Although the regional government would have the formal power implement mandatory sorting, the spaces and artefacts of the system are currently not able to handle large quantities of separate biowaste. In addition to the massive financial investment in new infrastructures that this would imply, modifying the existing rules has also political costs that incumbent decision-makers are apparently not willing to pay at present. This explains the recent and potentially temporary rule of biowaste sorting on a *voluntary* basis that Brussels has introduced all over its territory in 2017. After a successful communication campaign and an enthusiastic response from scores of superficially eco-conscious households, voluntary sorting now generates a biowaste flow that is sent in truck-loads to the biogas plant in Ypres. The environmental benefits of this operation are, however, rather dubious given that the trash collection trucks shuttling between Brussels and Ypres mainly transport water – and *more* non-recycled plastic bags. This being said, the voluntary sorting has the merit of allowing for more accurate estimates of biowaste flows that Brussels would have to manage once mandatory sorting will become operational.

Systemic representation

Figure 5.1 brings the different elements of this social-ecological system together. The graphical representation reflects the complexity of a system with different intertwined flows (water, faecal substances, food, energy, waste, etc.) and different treatment procedures (incineration, sewage, composting, biogas, etc.) that exist in parallel.

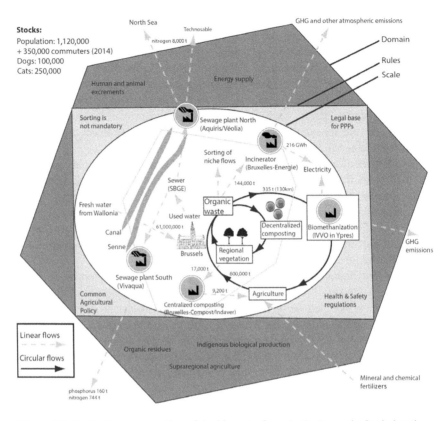

Figure 5.1 Systemic representation of the biowaste flows in the Brussels-Capital region.

Two flows are characterized by a certain circularity: on the one hand, a portion of the indigenous biomass production is metabolized through a polycentric network of composters and then returned to the regional ecosystem, thus forming a retroactive loop that increases biological productivity. The scale of these loops rarely surpasses municipal boundaries as input for the decentralized compost stations is typically sourced from a much smaller perimeter within the neighbourhood or even the same plot. On the other hand, a small fraction of biowaste (a few hundred tons) is collected separately through voluntary sorting and treated by anaerobic digestion in Ypres. This procedure is followed by the composting of the digestate (liquid remaining after anaerobic digestion). The compost is then reinjected into the agricultural system, which in turn produces foodstuff. The scale of this loop exceeds the Brussels metropolis: the household biowaste travels 130 km to Flanders and the green waste used in the composting of the digestate is sourced from ecosystems in Flanders.

Discussion of potential developments towards circular economy

According to the definition laid out earlier, a circular economy is a set of economic relationships that resembles the ideal-type of a waste-free, closed-loop system. Our rendering of the current system in Brussels illustrates that there are two alternative techniques that are associated with such circularity: both a treatment by anaerobic digestion and by decentralized composting converts into a resource what is today considered as waste. But the issues related to the circularization of waste are more encompassing than picking between two alternative technologies: any choice needs to take into account the interdependencies between technical artefacts and the other elements of the social-ecological system. A sizable change in the technical set-up will reflect the system's current domain, scale, rules, etc., but will also inevitably force these other elements to adapt in turn – a socio-technical interdependence described as "co-evolution" by Barles (2015). The way in which the social-ecological system co-evolves through time gives rise to alternative trajectories, and the challenge for rational policy-making boils down to choosing a trajectory with superior economic, social and environmental consequences.

We conclude this chapter with an exploratory and mainly qualitative evaluation of two contrasting trajectories that appear to be salient for the situation in Brussels: the first one is the industrial-scale deployment of anaerobic digestion in form of a single centralized treatment plant based on state-of-the-art technology; the second is the multiplication of decentralized composting stations.

"The third industrial revolution"

The centralized treatment of all biowaste from Brussels through anaerobic digestion would require the construction of one of the largest biogas plants in Europe, with a capacity of 5–7 MWh. Such a solution would be technologically complex and mainly rely on technological rather than social innovations. Several elements of the current configuration could be harnessed for implementing this trajectory, notably the rules underlying the subsidies to renewable energies (e.g. Feed-In Tariffs), the influence of multinational companies, the legal framework of PPPs and the current dominance of centralized industrial facilities that are still the business-as-usual solution to challenges of this kind.

Regarding the economic consequences, this is a solution that requires substantial up-front investment (probably more than 20 million euro), leading to an increase in public debt and creating a dozen or so of highly productive employments in the control and maintenance of an automated park of sophisticated machinery. If the subsidies to renewable energies are maintained, this trajectory would lead to profits captured by the consortium of companies charged with the construction and operation of the plant, as well as by the financial agents that provide the necessary capital. The formula of a "Third Industrial Revolution", often used by advocates of a tech-intensive variant of circular economy *à la*

McDonough and Braungart (2002), captures that this trajectory perpetuates the objective of economic growth and the increase of material throughput in the system. As in the incineration of waste, the operator of a new centralized facility would have no financial incentives to decrease the flows treated by the plant.

As for the social consequences, this trajectory is marked by a conception of the wider population reduced to a mass of passive consumers whose knowledge is not essential or even useful for the functioning of the system. The participation of the citizenry would be limited to sorting the household biowaste and to finance the operators through taxes or tariffs. By contrast, the biogas plant would require specialized knowledge held by experts, such as chemical engineers. This type of technical expertise is in general not related to the specificity of a given region.

The environmental impact of anaerobic digestion appears to be less negative compared to incineration. Moreover, it is a solution able to take in almost any type of biowaste including animal-related substances such as meat or dairy for which special regulations exist at the European level. A great environmental advantage is the possibility of converting the digestate into compost. The latter can be returned to agriculture and thereby close the loops of minerals that are contained in the urban biowaste stream. This being said, industrial methanization tends to produce an abundant stream of low-quality output, which explains that it meets very low demand from farmers (Brussels Environment 2015). For turning the entire digestate into compost, substantial quantities of dry organic matter would have to be imported from the countryside into the city of Brussels.

The polycentric alternative

The decentralized multiplication of collectively used compost sites would be a socially complex undertaking but represents relative minor technological challenges. This trajectory would extend the existing network of compost stations and could mobilize available knowledge from civic organizations, the 400 master composters that have already been trained over the last years and citizens that already engages with composting.

In economic terms, this trajectory is extremely labour-intensive but would required less capital outlays: we estimate that the treatment of 30,000 t/y of biowaste would need the involvement of 1,000 master composters and an investment of around 8.7 million euro for the (local) construction of 5,600 new stations. In the current decentralized organization of collection and treatment, the different tasks that are necessary for small-scale, low-tech composting are not remunerated, which actually reduces public expenditures by around 2,400 euro per year per master composter if we base the estimate on the net costs of a treatment by centralized biomethanization. Instead of using non-paid voluntary work, it would therefore be possible to compensate active citizens willing to perform some of the tasks of a decentralized composting system. According to our estimates, this compensation could equal up to 200 euro per month without exceeding the costs of the alternative industrial trajectory. In this case, decentralized composting would not create a salaried workforce, but rather a form of financially compensated civic action. It is important to stress that such a trajectory is a departure from the logic of economic growth through automation and augmentation of flows: it represents a localized manifestation of the alternative logic of post-growth that is the central theme of this book.

As for its social impact, the positive consequences of collective composting (social cohesion, participation, awareness raising, education, etc.) have been flagged by different studies and are subject to a large consensus (Ahoussoude *et al.* 2014; Brussels Environment 2015). We nevertheless stress that the trajectory outlined here would give rise to a form of polycentric and to a large extent self-organized form of resource management, which implies that it could benefit from the multiple advantages that have been associated with this management type in the literature on the adaptive governance of social-ecological systems (Dietz *et al.* 2003; Ostrom 2007, 2008). To illustrate these advantages with an example, the high physical, biological and chemical quality of neighbourhood composts that is typically attested by municipal screenings can be directly linked to the active participation of users and their understanding of the process of composting.

Finally, decentralized composting has both advantages and disadvantages in terms of its environmental consequences. A report by Brussels Environmental Agency from 2015 underlines the advantages by arguing that "it is the way of the least environmental impact because it requires no mechanical operation consuming energy, no collection or transportation and the compost produced by it is of high quality because it is directly used by its producer" (our translation). However, this quote also reveals the environmental disadvantages of polycentric composting because it does not foresee the return of mineral nutrients to agricultural fields. Closing the loop to agriculture would certainly require a closer cooperation between different compost stations as well as the creation of a mechanism to collect and transport the output to (peri-urban) fields. Two other environmental limits are the smaller spectrum of types of biowaste that can be treated through simple low-tech composting (for instance, animal-related substances cannot be treated due to regulatory barriers) and the upper limit of around 5,000 composters that is the consequence of the estimated amount of indigenous biological production of around 30,000 t/y that would need to be co-fed into the polycentric composting system to ensure a harmonious process of decomposition.

A hybrid solution needs to "hold together"

We have chosen deliberately to oppose two rather contrasting social-ecological trajectories. In practice, the system in Brussels and other cities with similarly configured systems (Paris, Montreal, London, etc.) could just as well evolve towards hybrid systems in which different options are combined, for instance by building several decentralized units of biomethanization and a semi-industrial composting plant. A hybrid trajectory combining centralized and decentralized elements and the co-existence of different treatment options not only appears as being the most likely in light of current political debates, but could also foster the diversity of solutions and thereby boost the resilience of the social-ecological system of Brussels.

Any combination of "industrial" and "post-growth" trajectories requires nevertheless that the partial implementation of each trajectory gives rise to a coherent whole. Brussels' pilot experiment with voluntary biowaste sorting followed by anaerobic digestion in Ypres shows that the two trajectories are not necessarily complementary: many citizens that have previously been active in bottom-up initiatives of self-organized composting have been converted back to behaving as passive consumers in a system that they don't understand.

Etymologically, the word "system" is rooted in the terms *syn* – meaning "together" – and *histanai* – "causing to stand". Any hybrid system of urban bio-waste management blending centralized, industrial-type solutions with decentralized, participatory strategies needs to ensure that the advantages of different solutions "stand together" as a system rather than undermine each other.

Acknowledgements

The author would like to thank Nicolas Scherrier, Patrick Van Den Abeele, Cédric Chevalier, Swen Ore, Bertrand Vanbelle, Laurent Dennemont et Stefan Döblin for their respective contributions to the research presented in this chapter.

Note

1 The remainder of the 30,000 t/y of green waste collected in Brussels is treated by the composting plan in Grimbergen.

References

Ahoussoude, G., Gossart, A., Moehler, K., Nyst, J., Progneaux, E., Wello, G. and Zouhair, M. (2014). *Comment repenser la gestion des déchets organiques ménagers et HoReCa dans la Région Bruxelles-Capitale?* IGEAT, Projet Interdisciplinaire Ii.

Arnsperger, C. and Bourg, D. (2016). Vers une économie authentiquement circulaire. *Revue de l'OFCE*, 1: 91–125.

Barles, S. (2010). Society, Energy and Materials: What are the Contributions of Industrial Ecology, Territorial Ecology and Urban Metabolism to Sustainable Urban Development Issues? *Journal of Environmental Planning and Management*, 53(4): 439–455.

Barles, S. (2015). The Main Characteristics of Urban Socio-Ecological Trajectories: Paris (France) from the 18th to the 20th Century. *Ecological Economics*, 118: 177–185.

Billen, G., Toussaint, F., Peeters, P., Sapir, M., Steenhout, A. and Vanderborght, J.P. (1983). *L'ecosysteme Belgique. Essai d'écologie industrielle*. Brussels: CRISP.

Bruno, I., Jany-Catrice, F. and Touchelay, B. (eds) (2016). *The Social Sciences of Quantification: From Politics of Large Numbers to Target-Driven Politics*. Switzerland: Springer.

Brussels Environnement (2015). *Métabolisme de la Région De Bruxelles-Capitale: Identification des flux, acteurs et activités économiques sur le territoire et pistes de réflexion pour l'optimisation des resources*. Rapport compilé par Batir, Ecores et ICEDD.

Dennemont, L. (2012). *La gestion des biodéchets à Bruxelles. Etat des lieux, analyse, perspectives.* Travail de fin de cycle, Centre universitaire de Charleroi.

Dietz, T., Ostrom, E. and Stern, P.C. (2003). The Struggle to Govern the Commons. *Science*, 302(5652): 1907–1912.

Duvigneaud, P. (1974). *La Synthèse écologique: Populations, communautés, écosystèmes, biosphère, noosphère.* Paris: Doin.

Duvigneaud, P. and Denayer-De Smet, S. (1975). L'ecosysteme Urbs. L'ecosysteme urbain Bruxellois. In P. Duvigneaud and P. Kestemont (eds), *Productivite biologique en Belgique.* Gembloux: Editions Duculot, pp. 581–597.

Ellen MacArthur Foundation and Granta Design (2015). *Circularity Indicators: An Approach to Measuring Circularity.* Report.

Fischer-Kowalski, M. and Haberl, H. (eds) (2007). *Socioecological Transitions and Global Change: Trajectories of Social Metabolism and Land Use.* Cheltenham: Edward Elgar.

Gallopoulos, N.E. (2006). Industrial Ecology: An Overview. *Progress in Industrial Ecology*, 3(1–2): 10–27.

Georgescu-Roegen, N. (1987). The Entropy Law and the Economic Process in Retrospect. *Schriftenreihe des IÖW*, 5/87: 4–31.

Holling, C. (2006). Shooting the Rapids: Navigating Transitions to Adaptive Governance of Socio-Ecological Systems. *Ecology and Society*, 11(1): 1–18.

Jonckhoff, E. and Van der Kooij, E. (2015). *Towards the Amsterdam Circular Economy.* City of Amsterdam's Physical Planning Department (DRO) and the Municipal Working Party for Materials.

Kampelmann, S. and De Muynck, S. (forthcoming). Les implications d'une circularisation des métabolismes territoriaux – une revue de la littérature. *Pour.*

Kohlbrenner, Ananda (2014). De l'engrais au déchet, des campagnes à la rivière: une histoire de Bruxelles et de ses excréments. *Brussels Studies*, 78, 23 June.

Lyle, John T. (1985). *Design for Human Ecosystems: Landscape, Land Use, and Natural Resources.* Washington, DC: Island Press.

McDonough, W. and Braungart, M. (2002). *Cradle to Cradle: Remaking the Way We Make Things.* New York: North Point Press.

McNeill, J.R. (2001). *Something New Under the Sun: An Environmental History of the Twentieth-Century World.* New York: W.W. Norton.

Ostrom, E. (2007). A Diagnositic Approach of Going Beyond Panaceas. *Proceeding of the National Academy of Sciences*, 104(39): 15181–15187.

Ostrom, E. (2008). Institutions and the Environment. *Economic Affairs*, 28(3): 24–31.

Ostrom, E. (2010). Beyond Markets and States: Polycentric Governance of Complex Economic Systems. *American Economic Review*, 100(3): 641–672.

Servigne, P. (2014). *Nourrir l'Europe en temps de crise.* Jambes: Editions Nature & Progrès.

Stahel, W. (2010). *The Performance Economy.* Basingstoke: Palgrave Macmillan.

Steffen, W., Richardson, K., Rockström, J., Cornell, S., Fetzer, I., Bennett, E., Biggs, R., Carpenter, S., De Vries, W., De Wit, C., Folke, C., Gerten, D., Heinke, J., Mace, G., Persson, L., Ramanathan, V., Reyers, B. and Sörlin, S. (2015). Planetary Boundaries: Guiding Human Development on a Changing Planet. *Science*, 347(6223): 736–746.

6 Ecological economics

Thinking of the post-growth era and its new sustainability indicators

Géraldine Thiry

The path towards a post-growth society is not yet marked out. We face huge uncertainties of a new kind: our development patterns are likely to jeopardize their own conditions of possibility. For Paul Crutzen, we enter into a new geological era where the impacts of mankind on the Earth's ecosystem are tremendous: the "anthropocene". "For three centuries, humanity's impact on the planetary environment has worsened. Because of anthropogenic carbon dioxide emissions, the Earth climate could significantly drift from its natural regime for the coming millennia" (Crutzen 2007: 143, our translation). Several studies suggest that the continued expansion of the human economy could lead to a catastrophic destabilization of the vital functions of the planet (see Farley *et al.* 2015). If, as Teilhard de Chardin (1966 [1923]) suggested at the beginning of the twentieth century with his concept of "noosphere", the human intellect has an increasing role to play in controlling its environment and its own future, it is crucial to identify the intellectual productions that are most likely to secure the future of our societies.

As far as economics is concerned, the question can be formulated that way: if economics (as a discipline) shapes the economy (as a system), what type of economics do we need in order to support the transition towards a post-growth society? With Spash (2011: 343), we consider that "serious attention to environmental reality leads to the need for a totally new way of thinking based on political economy and interdisciplinary learning". Following Einstein's famous formula, "we cannot solve our problems with the same thinking we used when we created them".

That is why rethinking economics in the perspective of a "post-growth society", which would be less reliant on market, more equitable and more respectful of nature than a "growth society", requires questioning the theoretical roots of neoclassical economics. With Söderbaum (1999, 2011, 2015) we believe that, like any other theoretical perspective in social science, neoclassical economics is a science as much as an ideology.[1]

Compared to other schools of thought, however, neoclassical economics noticeably dominates the collective imaginaries of most decision-makers (at the economic and political levels), and legitimizes their values, their ways of thinking and their behaviours. The pivotal role of markets in neoclassical economics, as analytical matrices and problem-solving tools, as well as the underlying onto-logical assumptions, where the individual is a utility-maximizing agent exclusively driven by an instrumental rationality, seem hardly compatible with the imperatives of a post-growth society.

Ecological economics, in its diversity and heterogeneity, appears much more promising to pave the way for a post-growth society. "The promise of ecological economics is that it will lead to an understanding of how to reconcile the economy with the biophysically limited planet in a way that other paradigms have not" (Krall and Klitgaard 2011: 185) It is, in our view, the renewal economic thinking needs, since ecological economics

> puts forward the idea that the environmental issue is not one question as another, that it leads to a crisis of mainstream economics and, in doing so, that it must lead to a profound questioning of its theoretical and conceptual frameworks.
>
> (Vivien 2007: 40, our translation)

We focus here on an area where ecological economics could play (and already plays) a transformative role: new indicators of sustainability. Indicators are multifaceted objects. They are often based on theoretical and methodological presuppositions and carry, accordingly, a specific epistemology. Indicators result from conventional choices which are historically, geographically and ideologically situated, and therefore crystallize different visions of the world. They also constitute political and normative guidelines (at different levels) by shedding light on some problems, and therefore potentially influence behaviours and decisions. The conceptual and normative underpinnings of indicators are thus essential elements to be taken into account for understanding the trajectory of a society that would use them as milestones to guide its choices.

In this chapter, we first present what distinguishes ecological economics from neoclassical economics: the integration of normativity, politics and ideology within the perimeter of scientificity. We then present three families of epistemological and methodological options that co-exist within ecological economics. For each of these trends within ecological economics, we draw an outline of the quantification options that are advocated and of the indicators (and forms of accounting) that are proposed. We will see that the importance of quantification slightly varies from one current to the other. We conclude with some consideration on the possibility, the desirability and the relevance of articulating all these different quantification options in the perspective of a post-growth society.

Ecological economics: when politics integrates science

Ecological economics is a school of thought whose outlines are still vague and moving. Ecological economics includes researchers whose methodological options diverge (sometimes radically), as we will see below. However, one important common feature links the diversity of works in ecological economics:

they are all explicitly committed to *normative objectives* that are recognized as part of any research process. Paradoxically, this common epistemological posture, which in our view is the strength of ecological economics, also explains its difficulty to set itself up as a school of economic thought in its own right.

A value-led rather than a method-led discipline

Ecological economists often identify themselves with different normative milestones that shape the outlines of their object of study and, more fundamentally, form the motive of their research. This was consubstantial to the creation of the movement: established in the late 1980s, ecological economics

> initially established itself as a research program lying at the intersection of the social and life sciences. It brought together people dissatisfied with these disciplines who agreed on several common goals: to take the problematic relationship between economic and natural systems seriously and to determine the conditions under which these systems could be "sustainable".
>
> (Merino-Saum and Roman 2014: 2)

From its origin, ecological economics aimed at promoting sustainability. In the first issue of *Ecological Economics*, Proops (1989) makes *measurement* and *policy* the two key objectives of ecological economics. Robert Costanza, for his part, defines ecological economics as "the science and management of sustainability". For Herman Daly, another figurehead in ecological economics, "we need a plan for remodeling the house we live in while we are living in it, so that it will conform as much as possible to the basic principles of a steady-state economy, without making us homeless in the meantime" (correspondence reported by Krall and Klitgaard 2011: 185). The common distinction between the positive and the normative is thus dissipated, in favour of a research approach explicitly guided by values and normative imperatives.

In doing so, the research programme of ecological economics is resolutely different from that of environmental economics that comes from neoclassical welfare economics. While neoclassical economics analyses the society–environment interactions through the prism of allocative efficiency, supposedly value-neutral – since normative questions are left outside the scope of economic analysis – ecological economics is shaped according to normative milestones where issues of *scale* and of *distribution* pre-empt the issue of resources allocation (Daly 1992). While they are careful of allocative efficiency and waste, ecological economists do not consider the market as the ultimate analytical matrix (we will see however that on the methodological level, some ecological economists mobilize the market tools in a pragmatic and instrumental perspective).

The main normative milestones that guide ecological economists are the interest in the sustainability of society–economy–nature interactions, societal resilience factors and distributional issues associated with ecological issues (environmental conflicts, access to resources, distribution of causes of environmental disturbances and impacted populations). Baumgärtner and Quaas (2010: 446) identify four core attributes to what they call sustainability economics:

1 subject focus on the relationship between humans and nature;
2 orientation towards the long-term and inherently uncertain future;
3 normative foundation in the idea of justice, between humans of present and future generations as well as between humans and nature;
4 concern for economic efficiency, understood as non-wastefulness, in the allocation of natural goods and services as well as their human-made substitutes and complements. Sustainability is the first objective, before efficiency.

Because it acknowledges the complexity of its object and the underlying radical uncertainty, ecological economics integrates normativity and values within the perimeter of scientificity. Once accepted the idea that uncertainty may not be controlled by science, the *motive* of scientific research is fundamentally altered:

> the scientific problems which are addressed can no longer be chosen on the basis of abstract scientific curiosity or industrial imperatives. Instead, scientists now tackle problems introduced through policy issues, where, typically, facts are uncertain, values in dispute, stakes high and decisions urgent.
>
> (Funtowicz and Ravetz 1991: 1381)

In that perspective, the economist is recognized as a political actor in his own right (Söderbaum 2015) because of his choice of subject, his analytical framework or his methodological options. The normativity of his approach is no longer separated from the perimeter of scientificity:

> As economists we should enter into an open dialogue about ideological orientations rather than argue that ideology is something to be left to politicians [...] If the dominance of specific ideologies connected with specific political parties is judged to be part of the problems faced then we cannot regard those ideologies as being outside the analysis.
>
> (Söderbaum 2015: 423)

A suitable posture for the search for new indicators

Recognizing uncertainty, values underlying scientific practice, and the existence of a plurality of legitimate perspectives (beyond those of the "experts"), ecological economics provides a suitable epistemological framework for the development of new indicators, in the perspective of a post-growth society. These three dimensions echo the different challenges encountered in the search for new indicators "beyond GDP".

First, the uncertainty characterizing the social and ecological impacts of human activity regularly gives rise to conflicts in the search for indicators of sustainability. This is illustrated, for example, in the third part of the Stiglitz Report:

In short, the global question we had to look at was to know whether some well-chosen statistics can tell us whether our children or grandchildren will face opportunities at least equivalent to the ones that we have had. In doing so, we have to take account of the large body of literature that has been already devoted to this topic. The problem in this field is not the lack of ideas. The problem is rather to understand why it seems so difficult to propose some federative indexes allowing a shared perception of whether our economies are sustainable or not.

(Stiglitz *et al.* 2009: 233)

Second, the issues of value underlying the sustainability indicators largely explain that no consensus on a new indicator – or set of indicators – emerges. Finally, the recognition of a plurality of legitimate perspectives is the *raison d'être* of numerous citizen movements such as the Forum for Other Indicators of Wealth in France (FAIR), whose members denounce the risk of technocratic appropriation of quantification and advocate more democratic procedures for developing indicators, which are considered as potential disciplinary devices (Foucault 1975) or tools of domination (Martuccelli 2010).

In terms of quantification, this reflexive posture implies assessing the indicator (or set of indicators) not only with respect to its internal logical validity, but rather to its external relevance:

An argument can be valid by the rules of logic and still have no connection with the real world; validity says nothing about truth content. When one moves from internal concerns to external matters attention shifts to the problem of concordance—how closely a model or theory corresponds to the world it purports to explain.

(Bromley 1990: 87)

Heterogeneity of quantification options

The fact that ecological economics is guided by normative concerns rather than by its own methods implies the co-existence of several currents whose methodological options strongly diverge. These discrepancies are particularly obvious in the way human–nature interactions are accounted for (through indicators or alternative forms of accounting). Indeed, in order to identify the conditions of sustainable societies and their compatibility with the physical limits of the planet, it is important to provide clear representations of the state of societies, ecosystems and the impacts of human activity on nature. The issue of indicators is therefore of tremendous importance for many the ecological economists and crystallizes their divergences. We distinguish three trends. We identify and classify those according to their degree of proximity to neoclassical economics. Note that these trends are neither mutually exclusive nor hermetic to one another. The main purpose of this typology is to clarify the presentation of the wide range of quantification options proposed.

Trend focused on "natural capital" and the assessment of ecosystem services

This trend tackles the problem of the biophysical limits through the lens of "natural capital" and ecosystem services. Its initial observation is that scarcity and/or degradation of ecosystem services is due (at least partly) to the lack of valorization of these services (Liu *et al.* 2010: 54).

This trend is the closest one to neoclassical economics. It conceives environmental problems as negative externalities, and applies the neoclassical methods commonly advocated for dealing with "market failures": assessing natural capital or ecosystem services consists in internalizing such externalities. This approach assumes that "with proper valuation markets will allocate efficiently on the basis of more accurate information about the true costs of economic activity" (Krall and Klitgaard 2011: 186).

The proponents of this trend, such as Robert Costanza or Pavan Sukhdev, are aware of the limitations of analyses carried out through the prism of the market. Endorsing this analytical framework is more a political choice, based on a good understanding of the power relations at stake as far as environmental policy is concerned: "Economic valuations [...] communicate the value of ecosystems and biodiversity and their largely unpriced flows of public goods and services in the language of the world's dominant economic and political model" (Sukhdev 2010: xxvii). Neoclassical economics' tools are thus mobilized for strategic and instrumental reasons: adopting the rhetoric which is most likely to be understood and listened to among the decision-makers. The extension of accounting to natural assets is a straightforward corollary of this posture (Folke *et al.* 1994).

The Economics of Ecosystems and Biodiversity (TEEB) is a concrete example of such endeavour and has a wide institutional visibility. The genesis of TEEB dates back to 2007, during the meeting of the G8+5 ministers of environment held in Potsdam. It was then proposed to undertake a wide-ranging study to assess the economic impacts of global biodiversity loss and to provide tangible economic arguments for conservation policies. This approach was inspired by the first "Stern Report" (Stern 2007), which mobilized economic analysis to motivate action (and quantify the cost of inaction) regarding climate change. TEEB was aimed at replicating this exercise for ecosystem services. It consists in a monetary accounting system designed to focus attention on the overall economic benefits of biodiversity and to highlight the increasing costs of biodiversity loss and ecosystems degradation. For Bartelmus (2010: 2054), "only monetary valuation provides the measuring rod for comparing the significance of environmental services with that of economic activity".

The opportunity and desirability of monetizing ecosystems have raised many debates among ecological economists. Three major families of criticisms (at least) are opposed to monetization. The first criticism refers to the lack of robustness and scientific credibility, especially when contingent valuation is the basis of monetary valuation (Gasparatos *et al.* 2008). A second important criticism has to do with the treatment of environmental problems as "externalities". This criticism being expressed by what we identify as the third trend of ecological economics, we will develop it below, in the section devoted to it. Finally, beyond the problems of scientific relevance, there is great concern among ecological economists that monetization induces a competitive logic, modifying the property rights of initially common resources and commodifying ecosystems (Gómez-Baggethun *et al.* 2010).

Trend focused on "steady-state economy"

The figureheads of this second trend are Herman Daly and Joshua Farley. As for the trend focused on "natural capital" and the assessment of ecosystem services, these authors stress the importance of extended accounting for natural capital. Unlike the first trend, however, this one directly questions the issue of economic growth and puts scale issues at the heart of its concerns.

For the proponents of this trend, a steady-state economy, that is, an economy which develops but without increasing its material size, is the best solution to current problems: "while growth must end, this in no way implies an end to development, which we define as qualitative change" (Daly and Farley 2004: 6). In the analytical framework proposed by Daly and Farley, the idea of developing without growth rests upon the distinction between three stakes: scale, distribution and allocation. Priority is given to the search for the optimal scale of economic activity and the intra- and intergenerational distribution of ecological resources. The economy is conceived as embedded in nature: "the larger the scale of the economy becomes, the greater the risk of destroying the conditions for human life on earth in the long run" (Røpke 2005: 275). Once limits to growth are acknowledged, the issue of distribution becomes tremendously important (Luks and Stewen 1999).

Once issues of scale and distribution are solved, then only can markets intervene to allocate resources. Tim Jackson (2009, 2017) popularized this vision, with his book *Prosperity Without Growth*. The pragmatic use of mainstream economics methods, combined with concerns regarding the optimal scale of the economy, has given rise to several types of quantification propositions. First, the ISEW (Index of Sustainable Economic Welfare), created by Daly and Cobb (1994 [1989]), and its close cousin the GPI (Genuine Progress Index; Cobb and Cobb 1994). These two synthetic monetary indicators, which are very similar, aim to better integrate the evolution of a country's well-being by taking into account the environmental and social dimensions that are absent from GDP: domestic work, non-defensive public expenditure, defensive private expenditure, environmental degradation and natural capital depletion. They are both adjusted to income inequalities. The longitudinal decoupling observed between ISEW and GDP in the United States has often been considered as the validation of the threshold hypothesis, according to which

> for every society there seems to be a period in which economic growth (as conventionally measured) brings about an improvement in the quality of

life, but only up to a point—the threshold point—beyond which, if there is more economic growth, quality of life may begin to deteriorate.

(Max-Neef 1995: 117)

Daly therefore speaks of "uneconomic growth" and supports the project of a steady-state economy. However, the validity of this decoupling (and hence of the threshold hypothesis) has been questioned. For Neumayer (2000), the occurrence of this decoupling is very sensitive to the methodological underpinnings of the ISEW, which according to him are based on a problematic theoretical basis in several respects: how non-renewable resources are evaluated; the valorization of long-term environmental damages; and how the indicator is adjusted to inequalities.

In addition to these composite indices, there are indicators of eco-efficiency. These indicators aim at responding to the questions: "Does the economy become more ecologically efficient?" or "Is the economy likely to produce more wealth or income with less material and/or energy resources?" Although these indicators do not reflect the absolute limits of the planet (since they are relative measures), they nevertheless provide useful information on the link between the economic activity and its material resources. They are expressed in units of energy or matter per unit of GDP (eco-efficiency) or, conversely, in GDP per unit of energy or matter (eco-productivity). Eco-efficiency objectives include "Factor 4" initiatives (Weizsäcker *et al.* 1997) or "Factor 10" (Schmidt-Bleek and Klüting 1994). The European Union has also adopted eco-productivity measures combining, amongst others, GDP with indicators of domestic material consumption (DMC). These indicators indicate the extent to which the economy is "dematerialized", or follows a "green growth" trajectory. They should not, however, divert attention from objectives in absolute terms, which are more ecologically meaningful (Jackson 2017).

A third type of indicator encompasses indicators of energy and materials flows (Fischer-Kowalski *et al.* 2011). Unlike eco-efficiency indicators, the flow indicators are expressed exclusively in physical units of account. The primary purpose of these indicators is to account for the size of the social metabolism of the economy. The question of scale is therefore at the heart of their methodology. These indicators have the advantage (among other things) of relying on categories compatible with those of the national accounts, which makes it possible to integrate physical and monetary information into the same accounting framework: "Considering the gross domestic product (GDP) of a country alongside its material use enables countries to monitor their progress in decoupling resource use from economic growth" (Fischer-Kowalski *et al.* 2011: 2).

Finally, let us mention a last type of indicator that could be connected to this trend of ecological economics: the "sustainability gaps" (Ekins and Simon 2001). Sustainability gaps compare environmental performances with sustainability standards. These standards are defined according to principles that respect a clear distinction between two types of functions that nature provides:

"functions for", which provide direct benefits to humans, and "functions of", which maintain the integrity of natural systems. The continuous working of the "functions of" is a necessary condition for the continuity of "functions for" humans. Once the ecological standards have been defined, it is possible to calculate the sustainability gaps, understood as the difference between these standards and the current state of the environment (or the pressures exerted on it). These gaps can be expressed in physical terms (e.g. greenhouse gas emissions), monetary (costs to achieve the target) or sustainability years (number of years required to reach the target).

Social ecological economics

The first two trends presented are mostly rooted in the United States. We identify a third trend, whose members (Bina Agarwal, Joan Martinez-Alier, Richard Norgaard, Clive Spash, Peter Söderbaum and John Gowdy are among the best known) belong mostly to the European fringe of ecological economics. While this trend shares Daly's (1992) concerns about scale and distribution issues, it is often more alarmist, more explicit about its deeply political and militant nature, and openly criticizes neoclassical economics.

This trend is linked to political ecology and is very interested in socio-ecological conflicts (Martinez-Alier 2014). Spash (2011) groups under the name of social ecological economics initiatives taking an interdisciplinary and resolutely heterodox approach to the interactions between economy and nature. At the ideological level, social ecological economics deals with problems requiring behavioural and systemic change (economic growth being unsustainable while still remaining pivotal in our societies), puts strong emphasis on issues of poverty and distribution, takes into account the state of power relations (at the individual, collective, political and company levels) at different scales (from local to international), considers markets as social constructions, develops alternative institutions, promotes participation, and recognizes that power issues are necessary to address the science–policy interface. Methodologically, the distinctive characteristics of social ecological economics include: axiological pluralism, recognition of incommensurability, interdisciplinarity, empiricism (using qualitative and quantitative methods), reluctance regarding the alleged rigour of mathematical formalism and recognition of radical uncertainty (ignorance and social indetermination).

In terms of quantification, several characteristics distinguish this current: refusal to analyse environmental issues in terms of externalities; strong reluctance (or even, for many, a firm opposition) to monetization, linked to the recognition of incommensurability; political rather than an economic ontology, underlying a strong social constructivism.

Common (2011) considers that apprehending environmental issues in terms of "externalities" is inappropriate for understanding the dynamics of complex adaptive systems. In a complex and evolving world, externalities are very difficult to evaluate. And even if they could, Common says, the allocative efficiency of markets (the normative horizon of neoclassical economics) would not guarantee the sustainability of development. More fundamentally, for Karl William Kapp (1950) and for many social ecological economists after him, externalities are not "external" to the market, but rather an inherent characteristic of the market. It is important for these authors to abandon the rhetoric of "externalities", which tends to consider uncompensated side effects as exceptional rather than pervasive, as accidental rather than systemic. For this trend, the analysis in terms of externalities and cost-shifting insidiously contributes to maintain the existing economic and social structure, to establish the status quo. However, in capitalist market economies, externalities are widespread, structural and chronic. As Krall and Klitgaard (2011) point out, these criticisms do not denounce a mere evaluation problem, but the fact that the structural foundations of capitalist market economies may per se not be compatible with the biophysical and ecological limits of the planet, and that the only way to cope with these limits is to change the structure of the economy itself.

Conceptions of the environment in terms of externalities are strongly linked to monetary valuation of nature (see Bithas 2011), which is criticized by the great majority of social ecological economists. Thus, for example, if Baumgärtner and Quaas (2010) promote the development of green accounting and "meaningful" indicators, they reject monetization. Considering the monetary valuation of ecosystem services, Norgaard (2010) denounces the drift of what was originally a metaphor that aimed to open the eyes of a broad public about the importance of nature and its destruction. For him, monetary valuation has become a dominant model in environmental management and policies:

> The metaphor's ties to the problems of continued global economic growth have largely been broken. Indeed, through carbon offsets and optimizing the use of ecosystem services in poor countries, the delusion of continuing consumption along its old path in the rich countries is being sustained.
>
> (Noorgard 2010: 1219)

The rejection of monetization is more fundamentally linked to the recognition of incommensurability. The adoption of a single comparison term, as is the case in monetization, presupposes strong commensurability of the variables. According to this assumption, all forms of capital (social, human, product or environmental) are perceived as strongly comparable, that is, they share common characteristics, whether or not they have a common denominator. Strong commensurability implies an axiological monism, which is hardly appropriate to grasp the complex stakes of sustainability:

> to hold that values are strongly commensurable is to hold not only that the measure ranks objects, but that there is a particular single property that all objects possess which is a source of their value, and that our evaluative measure indicates the amount or degree to which that property is present.
>
> (O'Neill 1993: 99)

Finally, strong commensurability is a necessary condition (though not sufficient) to substitutability between different forms of capital, which denies the existence of critical thresholds.

Therefore, to quantify human–nature interactions, social ecological economics favour multicriteria analyses (Munda *et al.* 1994; Munda 2008). Based on the observation that the analysis of environmental problems is mainly affected by conflicts related to technical, socio-economic, environmental and political value judgements, Munda *et al.* (1994) stress how hard it is to achieve an unambiguous solution for environmental management. Rather, they propose to seek for an acceptable compromise between the various interests involved. Such an exercise requires an appropriate methodology: the multicriteria analysis seems to be the most successful.

> The basic idea of multi-criteria evaluation is that in evaluation problems, we have first to establish objectives, that is, the direction of the desired changes of the world (e.g. maximize economic performance, minimize environmental impact, minimize social exclusion) and then find useful practical indicators (called criteria) which measure if the options considered are consistent with the objectives chosen.
>
> (Munda 2015: 405)

In the same vein, Söderbaum (1982) proposes the methodology of "positional analysis" to deal with multi-actor and multicriteria problems and to account for the plurality of visions on socio-environmental issues.

These different initiatives share a deeply political ontology, contrasting with the neoclassical *homo economicus*. Social ecological economists consider that the analytical framework of neoclassical economics is insufficient to address issues of justice and fundamental questions such as "what is nature?" or "what is the economy?" This constructivist perspective places institutions at the heart of collective choices: they are intrinsically linked to the way in which deliberative processes are settled. Depending on whether the deliberation method mobilizes the "consumer-self" (as in contingent valuation methods, for example) or the "citizen-self", as in a process of citizen deliberation, judgements that emerge are very different (Sagoff 1988; Soma and Vatn 2014; Zografos and Howarth 2008). Most social ecological economists agree with Mary Douglas (1986: 124, cited in Gowdy and Erickson 2005) who states that: "The most profound decisions about justice are not made by individuals as such, but by individuals within and on behalf of institutions."

Evaluation of the different options

The brief account of the different trends of ecological economics has highlighted the variety of quantification proposals to account for the interactions between economy, society and nature. A fault-line appears quite clearly between, on the one hand, those who advocate a fundamental and structural change in the system, which would involve a break with the dominant way of thinking, and on the other hand, a strategic posture aimed at bringing nature into decision-making, adopting the rhetoric and analytical tools of neoclassical economics. Are these two postures, at the extremes of a more complex continuum, reconcilable or, on the contrary, essentially incompatible?

Spash (2011: 366) considers them irreconcilable, and even mutually destructive. For him, those who adopt the analyses and positions of the neoclassical economics:

> may regard themselves as being pragmatic, in the sense of achieving an end by the easiest available means, but actually have created problems for those trying to be far more grounded in terms of changing economic thinking. Indeed, much of the ecosystems services valuation work, for example, merely buys into an existing political economy in which no substantive effort is on the agenda for challenging the idea that material and energy growth can continue ad infinitum. At the same time this work undercuts alternative efforts [...] not least by pretending that producing simple money numbers is a politically adequate response to global environmental problems.

If we share the fears pointed out by Spash, we think it might be more constructive to explore the conditions under which the articulation of the different proposals could mark a transition to a post-growth society. By definition, a transition is projected onto different time horizons, each with its constraints and possibilities. It seems to us that, to make an analogy with Fernand Braudel's (1979) "*étagement* of three temporalities" (long duration, conjunctures and present time), the different quantification options proposed by ecological economics must be thought of and articulated according to distinct and connected temporalities.

In the short term, although we share the reluctance of social ecological economics as far as the monetization of the environment is concerned, we may wonder if nature would be better taken into account in the absence of such monetary accounting. We can doubt that. To infiltrate the dominant forms of rationality by integrating nature into a set of cost–benefit analyses seems the most realistic means in the short term to make nature "exist" (in a very fragmentary and deeply instrumental way) in the field of decision-making. However, this means of action will not raise consciousness, will not shed light on the systemic and structural elements of unsustainability, and even if not hampered, may legitimize the perpetuation of the current system while eluding the stakes of planetary limits and of social justice.

If monetization is a short-term strategic tool, it must at the outset be imperatively framed and counterbalanced by other forms of quantification. Indicators such as, for example, eco-efficiency and eco-productivity measures seem promising in this respect. Their evolution over time is likely to report the progress made in the (relative) dematerialization of economies. To take up the analogy with the temporalities of Braudel, by highlighting the materiality of our modes of development, these indicators are likely to show the potential drifts, in the medium term, of perpetuating the current system (without however identifying the fundamental determinants).

In a long-term perspective, changes will have to take place at a more fundamental level. And the multicriteria evaluations suggested by the social ecological economics, if their practice is generalized from today on, seem the most able to generate them. By their participatory dimension, this type of analysis does not make the indicator a goal but rather a means of debating the values and conceptions of various societal actors. If they are based on appropriate institutional forms, shaped to awaken the consciousness of the collective rather than individual rationality, and highlighting the structural stakes necessary for the sustainability of life on earth, these deliberative processes have a real potential of transformation. Multicriteria assessments, because they can contribute to the internalization of each of the (individual and collective) conditions of postgrowth, help to strengthen the resilience of societies by consolidating the collective.

Note

1 Ideology is understood in the sense of Douglas North (1990) as a set of subjective perceptions (models, theories) that each individual has to explain the world. Whether at the level of individual relations or at the level of organized ideologies that provide global explanations of the past and the present (such as communism or religions), the "theories" that individuals shape are tainted by their normative visions on how the world should be organized.

References

Bartelmus, P. (2010). Use and Usefulness of Sustainability Economics. *Ecological Economics*, 69(11): 2053–2055.

Baumgärtner, S. and Quaas, M. (2010). What is Sustainability Economics? *Ecological Economics*, 69(3): 445–450.

Bithas, K. (2011). Sustainability and Externalities: Is the Internalization of Externalities a Sufficient Condition for Sustainability? *Ecological Economics*, 70(10): 1703–1706.

Braudel, F. (1979). *Civilisation matérielle, économie et capitalisme, XVe et XVIIe siècle.* Paris: Armand Collin.

Bromley, D.W. (1990). The Ideology of Efficiency: Searching to a Theory of Policy Analysis. *Journal of Environmental Economics and Management*, 19: 86–107.

Cobb, C.W. and Cobb, J.B. (1994). *The Green National Product: A Proposed Index of Sustainable Economic Welfare.* Lanham: University Press of America.

Common, M. (2011). The Relationship between Externality, and its Correction, and Sustainability. *Ecological Economics*, 70(3): 453.

Crutzen, P. (2007). La géologie de l'humanité : l'Anthropocène. *Ecologie & politique*, 34(1): 141–148.

Daly, H.E. (1992). Allocation, Distribution, and Scale: Towards an Economics that is Efficient, Just, and Sustainable. *Ecological Economics*, 6(3): 185–193.

Daly, H.E. and Cobb, J.B. (1994 [1989]). *For the Common Good: Redirecting the Economy toward Community, the Environment, and a Sustainable Future*. Boston: Beacon Press.

Daly, H.E. and Farley, J. (2004). *Ecological Economics: Principles and Applications*. Washington, Covelo and London: Island Press.

Douglas, M. (1986). *How Institutions Think*. Syracuse: Syracuse University Press.

Ekins, P. and Simon, S. (2001). Estimating Sustainability Gaps: Methods and Preliminary Applications for the UK and the Netherlands. *Ecological Economics*, 37(1): 5–22.

Farley, J., Schmitt, A., Burke, M. and Farr, M. (2015). Extending Market Allocation to Ecosystem Services: Moral and Practical Implications on a Full and Unequal Planet. *Ecological Economics*, 117: 244–252.

Fischer-Kowalski, M., Krausmann, F., Giljum, S., Lutter, S., Mayer, A., Bringezu, S. and Weisz, H. (2011). Methodology and Indicators of Economy-wide Material Flow Accounting: State of the Art and Reliability Across Sources. *Journal of Industrial Ecology*, 15(6): 855–876.

Folke, C., Hammer, M., Costanza, R. and Jansson, A. (1994). Investing in Natural Capital: Why, What, and How? In A. Jansson, M. Hammer, C. Folke and R. Costanza (eds), *Investing in Natural Capital: The Ecological Economics Approach to Sustainability*. Washington, DC: Island Press, pp. 1–20.

Foucault, M. (1975). *Surveiller et Punir. Naissance de la prison*. Paris: Gallimard.

Funtowicz, S. and Ravetz, J. (1991). A New Scientific Methodology for Global Environmental Issues. In R. Costanza (ed.), *Ecological Economics: The Science and Management of Sustainability*. Columbia: Columbia University Press, pp. 137–152.

Gasparatos, A., El-Haram, M. and Horner, M. (2008). A Critical Review of Reductionist Approaches for Assessing the Progress towards Sustainability. *Environmental Impact Assessment Review*, 28(4–5): 286–311.

Gómez-Baggethun, E., de Groot, R., Lomas, P.L. and Montes, C. (2010). The History of Ecosystem Services in Economic Theory and Practice: From Early Notions to Markets and Payment Schemes. *Ecological Economics*, 69(6): 1209–1218.

Gowdy, J. and Erickson, J.D. (2005). The Approach of Ecological Economics. *Cambridge Journal of Economics*, 29(2): 207–222.

Jackson, T. (2009). *Prosperity without Growth: Economics for a Finite Planet*. London: Earthscan.

Jackson, T. (2017). *Prosperity without Growth: Foundations for the Economy of Tomorrow*. London: Routledge.

Kapp, K.W. (1950). *The Social Costs of Private Enterprise*. Cambridge, MA: Harvard University Press.

Krall, L. and Klitgaard, K. (2011). Ecological Economics and Institutional Change. *Annals of the New York Academy of Sciences*, 1219(1): 185–196.

Liu, S., Costanza, R., Farber, S. and Troy, A. (2010). Valuing Ecosystem Services: Theory, Practice, and the Need for a Transdisciplinary Synthesis. *Annals of the New York Academy of Sciences*, 1185(1): 54–78.

Luks, F. and Stewen, M. (1999). Why Biophysical Assessments Will Bring Distribution Issues to the Top of the Agenda. *Ecological Economics*, 29(1): 33–35.

Martinez-Alier, J. (2014). *L'écologisme des pauvres une étude des conflits environnementaux dans le monde*. Paris: Les Petits Matins.

Martuccelli, D. (2010). Critique de la philosophie de l'évaluation. *Cahiers Internationaux de Sociologie*, 128–129: 27–52.

Max-Neef, M. (1995). Economic Growth and Quality of Life: A Threshold Hypothesis. *Ecological Economics*, 15(2): 115–118.

Merino-Saum, A. and Roman, P. (2014) What Can We Learn from Ecological Economics? *Books and Ideas*. Available online at: www.booksandideas.net/What-Can-We-Learn-From-Ecological.html.

Munda, G. (2008). *Social Multi-Criteria Evaluation for a Sustainable Economy*. New York: Springer.

Munda, G. (2015). Beyond GDP: An Overview of Measurement Issues in Redefining "Wealth". *Journal of Economic Surveys*, 29(3): 403–422.

Munda, G., Nijkamp, P. and Rietveld, P. (1994). Qualitative Multicriteria Evaluation for Environmental Management. *Ecological Economics*, 10(2): 97–112.

Neumayer, E. (2000). On the Methodology of ISEW, GPI and Related Measures: Some Constructive Suggestions and Some Doubt on the "Threshold" Hypothesis. *Ecological Economics*, 34(3): 347–361.

Norgaard, R.B. (2010). Ecosystem Services: From Eye-Opening Metaphor to Complexity Blinder. *Ecological Economics*, 69(6): 1219–1227.

North, D. (1990). *Institutions, Institutional Change and Economic Performance*. Cambridge: Cambridge University Press.

O'Neill, J. (1993). *Ecology, Policy, and Politics: Human Well-Being and the Natural World*. London and New York: Routledge.

Proops, J.L.R. (1989). Ecological Economics: Rationale and Problem Areas. *Ecological Economics*, 1(1): 59–76.

Røpke, I. (2005). Trends in the Development of Ecological Economics from the Late 1980s to the Early 2000s. *Ecological Economics*, 55(2): 262–290.

Sagoff, M. (1988). *The Economy of the Earth*. Cambridge: Cambridge University Press.

Schmidt-Bleek, F. and Klüting, R. (1994). *Wieviel Umwelt braucht der Mensch? MIPS – das Maß für ökologisches Wirtschaften*. Berlin: Birkhäuser.

Söderbaum, P. (1982). Positional Analysis and Public Decision Making. *Journal of Economic Issues*, 16(2): 391–400.

Söderbaum, P. (1999). Values, Ideology and Politics in Ecological Economics. *Ecological Economics*, 28(2): 161–170.

Söderbaum, P. (2011). Sustainability Economics as a Contested Concept. *Ecological Economics*, 70(6): 1019–1020.

Söderbaum, P. (2015). Varieties of Ecological Economics: Do We Need a More Open and Radical Version of Ecological Economics? *Ecological Economics*, 119: 420–423.

Soma, K. and Vatn, A. (2014). Representing the Common Goods: Stakeholders vs. Citizens. *Land Use Policy*, 41: 325–333.

Spash, C.L. (2011). Social Ecological Economics: Understanding the Past to See the Future. *American Journal of Economics and Sociology*, 70(2): 340–375.

Stern, N. (2007). *The Economics of Climate Change: The Stern Review*. Cambridge: Cambridge University Press.

Stiglitz, J.E., Sen, A. and Fitoussi, J.-P. (2009). *Rapport de la Commission sur la mesure des performances économiques et du progrès social*.

Sukhdev, P. (2010). Preface. In P. Kumar (ed.), *The Economics of Ecosystems and Biodiversity (TEEB)*. London: Earthscan, pp. xvii–xxvii.

Teilhard de Chardin, P. (1966 [1923]). *The Vision of the Past*. New York: Harper and Row, Publishers.

Vivien, F.-D. (2007). Economie de l'environnement ou économie écologique? *Responsabilité et Environnement*, 48: 37–43.

Weizsäcker, E.U. von, Lovins, A.B. and Lovins, L.H. (1997). *Factor Four: Doubling Wealth, Halving Resource Use: The New Report to the Club of Rome*. London: Earthscan.

Zografos, C. and Howarth, R.B. (eds) (2008). *Deliberative Ecological Economics*. New Delhi: Oxford University Press.

7 The cage and the labyrinth
Escaping the addiction to growth

Olivier De Schutter

The objective of growth, defined as the increase of GDP per capita, has been central to the macroeconomic policies of industrialized countries since this measure was initially introduced in the 1940s (Daly 1996). Beyond the mere convenience of this measure of progress, there are three reasons why it has been so successful. The two first reasons are strictly economic in nature. First, the more wealth creation expands, the more we can hope to create jobs and thus compensate, in part at least, the destruction of existing occupations, in the least advanced sectors of the economy, that follow from the increases in labour productivity associated with technological advances and the improvement of human capital. Second, growth makes the burden of the public debt, which has significantly risen since the oil crisis of 1973 and the subsequent economic crisis, more sustainable. This is of course for reasons of public accounting: the debt weighs less heavily on the public budget if the budget grows, in proportion of the increase in wealth creation. But in addition, economic growth allows the state to increase its revenues through various forms of taxation: the state needs citizens who recognize its legitimacy, but it also requires taxpayers who can be made to contribute to the financing of public goods.

Finally, a third reason why GDP growth per capita has been so popular as the dominant measure of progress is more strictly political in nature: the promise of growth in wealth creation is the promise of gradual increases in material prosperity, allowing the average person to consume more, without such increases having to depend on the state adopting strong redistributive policies. The so-called "Fordist" compromise, a central component of the reigning order of the post-Second World War era, was based on this idea: by the magic of economic growth, each generation could hope to attain a standard of living higher than that of the earlier generation, even within the lowest income quintiles of the population, without such a result having to depend on social policies designed to achieve a significant reduction of income inequalities. The quest for growth, in other terms, functioned in effect in the mainstream discourse as a substitute for more vigorous efforts towards social justice.

These justifications for growth, however, are grounded in turn on representations that run deeper, although they are rarely made explicit. These representations concern both the trajectory of the individual and that of society as a whole.

From the point of view of the individual, what is implicit in the myth of growth (Méda 2013) is that the flourishing of each member of society depends on the constant expansion of the possibilities of material consumption (Layard 2005; Dolan *et al.* 2008; Scitovsky 1976). It is this belief that makes it appear so imperative to strive for an increase in incomes combined with a reduction of the real price of consumer items, the latter being achieved thanks to the standardization of production and the competition between producers. It is this belief too, or this myth, that explains why the social status of the individual is made to depend on his or her access to some remunerative form of employment. Work is both a source of income, opening up the possibility of consumption, and a means of integration within society: it is through work that one can hope to achieve some form of social recognition. From the point of view of society as a whole, behind the myth of growth lurks the idea of an uninterrupted form of progress, following a timeline that leads us towards the "always more".

Happiness of the individual through consumption, and progress of society by the continued improvement of standards of living: it is these representations, or these myths, that are the main obstacles to the imagination of alternatives. *Autonomy* therefore emerges as a condition for such alternatives to emerge, and it is because they may favour such autonomy that the establishment of new modes of governance is key to the establishment of conditions that may lead to a shift to a society that would not have growth as its ultimate horizon – ultimate, and in practice almost exclusive. Autonomy, indeed, is the ability for the individual as well as for the community to choose the norms by which they shall be guided (Castoriadis 1975). Its exercise requires that we create the conditions for a sufficient reflexivity, allowing both the individual and society to define their long-term goals, and to make choices that shall allow them to make progress towards realizing those objectives. Ultimately, autonomy is about escaping the economicism characteristic of our advanced capitalist societies, i.e. the tendency to give priority to objectives of an economic nature, at the expense of other objectives such as, at the individual level, the "good life" (the *eudaimonia* in classic Greece), and at the societal level, resilience to future shocks or the creation of conditions that would favour the flourishing of the members of the community. Individual and collective autonomy should allow to redefine the significance of economic prosperity, understood as the extension of the possibilities of material consumption, and of its rank in our order of priorities: instead of being an end in itself, economic prosperity should become a means in the service of ends that we should choose freely (Cassiers 2015).

In order to make progress towards identifying the mechanisms that could make such a transformation possible, we must first understand the nature of the trap that has closed upon us. Where does this lack of imagination come from, which leads individuals and communities to become unable to think a horizon other than that of a never-ending quest for more growth, and to see any competing objective as of comparatively minor weight? This chapter suggests that the situation we inherit from is the result of an interaction between changes in the behaviour of the individual and the responses to such changes that have co-evolved at societal level.

It briefly discusses the terms of this interaction, which defines the cage in which we are imprisoned. It then addresses a second characteristic of our predicament: even as, within a small fraction of the opinion, the impasses resulting from the blind and never-ending pursuit of economic growth are gradually being acknowledged, the means to move away from these impasses remain vague and contested. We are prisoners of an inherited system, and although a growing number of people understand the need to escape from the religion of growth, they disagree as to the exit strategies that should be pursued – indeed, they disagree even on the very suggestion that a "strategy" is what we currently require. This should not be seen as a problem; rather, it should be considered a promise. We can only hope to escape the cage by accepting that the transition supposes a plurality of solutions, and by encouraging the search for many escape routes that should be explored simultaneously. We are in a cage, perhaps, but we are not prisoners of a labyrinth that would only allow for one exit route: it is starting from this dual characteristic of the present situation that we can reflect on the governance mechanisms that should be established to prepare the post-growth society.

The cage

From the point of view of the individual's behaviour, it is from the middle of the eighteenth century that we can date the emergence of what R. Tawney would call the acquisitive mentality (Tawney 1920; Laval 2007). At its origin, before its broader diffusion – diffusion both across larger parts of the population (beyond the class of merchants) and beyond the sphere of commerce alone (to gradually colonize other spheres of life) – this acquisitive mentality took the form of the domination of a specifically instrumental mode of rationality, of an accounting type, in which the individual seeks to compute the costs and benefits of each of his or her individual actions and to maximize gains while minimizing losses. It is by the rise of this calculating rationality that Max Weber defines the emergence of the spirit of capitalism (Weber 1992).

Of course, technological advances, the rational administration of justice by specialized public servants guaranteeing a stable legal framework and thus favouring the predictability of economic life, the emergence of the limited liability corporation, as well as the religious legitimation provided by the theory of predestination, all played a role in this development (Berman 1983). These various factors would not have produced the consequences they did in fact entail, however, if they have not been supported and relied upon by a class of economic actors obsessively seeking to maximize their gains and developing a permanent search for new forms of profit-making. It is this that characterizes the birth of the spirit of capitalism as such: not only the material gains obtained through "freedom" of exchange (which is at the heart of capitalism as an economic system that prioritizes market exchanges over the central command of the state), but also the infinite quest of material gain as an objective to which the whole life plans of the individual are dedicated (wherein lies the specifically psychological dimension of the capitalist economy).

The spirit of capitalism: the shaping of society by the individual

It is well known how, in *The Protestant Ethics and the Spirit of Capitalism*, Weber describes the trap that has closed upon us (Weber 1999). Once a small number of actors dedicate themselves to profit maximization, all the other actors are forced to adapt, by a process of *economic selection* that Weber explicitly analogizes to the process of natural selection described (though not labelled as such) by Charles Darwin half a century earlier: if the other economic actors did not also adopt the same kind of behaviour, they would risk being eliminated, not because of their lesser "intrinsic worth", but because they would be less competitive on the market. It is thus that, according to Weber, capitalism, "which has ensured its supremacy in economic life, educates and produces for itself, through economic selection, the economic subjects – the entrepreneurs and the workers – which it requires" (Weber 1999: 94). The result of this process is that capitalism, now that it is victorious – having vanquished all the competing models of organizing economic life – can dispense with the religious justification that may have originally favoured its ascendancy: with the division of labour, its "mechanical basis" has been radically transformed, creating the conditions of a mutual interdependance and of a generalized competition, to the point that there is no evident escape route left (Weber 1999: 301). We have lost the key of the prison that we have built around us.

We are caught in a double trap. The first is that the individual, left to him- or herself, cannot escape from the capitalist economic order: in order for such an escape to be possible, a collective action is required.

> Today, the capitalist economic order is a huge *cosmos* in which the individual is trapped from birth: this *cosmos* is for him a given, a straightjacket which that individual cannot transform, at least on his own, and within which he is forced to live.
>
> (Weber 1999: 93–94)

This is because it is only by dedicating oneself entirely to the accumulation of wealth that one can survive in the face of competition, in a world dominated by the spirit of capitalism: "Those who do not adapt their life patterns to the conditions of capitalist success drown or fail to emerge victorious" (Weber 1999: 117).

The second trap results from the addiction to work, and to the quest for "always more", which the immersion in such an economic order leads to. Weber remarks how it is deeply "irrational, from the point of view of individual happiness, to lead a life in which man exists for his work rather than the opposite", noting that if we asked these "natures eager for action" – we, who are motivated by the search for material gain – about the "'meaning' of their quest, which never allows them to be satisfied with what they own [...] they would typically answer [...] that their business and the constant dedication to work have become 'indispensable ingredients of their life'" (Weber 1999: 115). Ultimately therefore, what the individual is most handicapped by in capitalism, is a failure of the imagination: an inability to conceive of another way to give meaning to his existence, and to occupy his life.[1] That, however, is not all. For the individual's addiction to work also reflects the expectations of the other members of the community, who rather than treating it as a pathology or as betraying a lack of culture, value positively the accumulation of wealth. As noted by Weber, in terms that echo his contemporaries Veblen or Tawney (Veblen 1899; Tawney 1920): "when the imagination of all a people is drawn towards a purely quantitative form of value [...] this romanticism of the numbers exerts a magical and irresistable fascination on those of the merchants who are 'poets'" (Weber 1999: 115).

The society of generalized competition: the shaping of the individual by society

Such is the failure of the imagination: it is the inability for the individual to seek forms of happiness which have their source elsewhere than in the promise of wealth accumulation, which is sought after both for its presumed intrinsic value and because it distinguishes the successful as those who have proven to be capable of surviving the economic competition. As such, it is a failure of the individual. But a number of mechanisms established at societal level ensure that we, as individuals, are essentially programmed to fail. It is a troubling paradox that the first of these mechanisms, and probably the most decisive, is an idea which is at the heart of modernity, and one of its most stellar and uncontested achievements: the recognition that we are all equals. Indeed, as the ranking of individuals in the social order depends less, at least in principle, on the circumstances of their birth, we gradually have had to move to other marks of distinction, and material success has largely played this substituting role. One was classified by the pedigree of one's origins; one now is ranked by how much wealth one was able to accumulate, especially where such wealth is not inherited but is the result of one's efforts or of one's wisdom in making investments. "X is worth Y millions according to Forbes": ordinary language, here as elsewhere, is an almost explicit admission of the changed mores of the times. This means of ranking individuals, however, is a major obstacle to the emergence of life choices that move us away from our obsession with growth.

Other mechanisms concern the economic institutions, and the incentives they provide respectively for entrepreneurs, workers and consumers. Entrepreneurs are encouraged to permanently innovate and to improve the efficiency of production, by the generalized competition that is imposed on them – further strengthened by the lowering of obstacles to regional and international trade – never mind if such efficiency gains are often illusory, when they are based on the ability to impose on the collectivity social costs (the so-called negative externalities, in Pigovian terms) that are not incorporated in the costs of production. Workers are incentivized to permanently improve their qualifications: idleness is suspect, and since wage losses are compensated by unemployment benefits or by social aid, the members of the active population who are unemployed are encouraged to project themselves as potential economic agents – capable, through certain efforts, to provide for themselves. Therefore, although there is less employment available than in the past, we continue to define full-time and lifelong employment as the necessary horizon of our individual trajectories, without in any way encouraging individuals to think about other useful ways to occupy the time freed up by the impressive gains of labour productivity: the so-called "activation" of social benefits is the most striking symptom of this collective blindspot (De Schutter 2015). Consumers, finally, are subjected to the relentless propagandizing from the advertising industry, which somehow manages to convince the members of the public that they have large numbers of unsatisfied wants they were unaware of, and that any of their desires should be treated as urgent needs; consumers which in turn rank themselves according to lifestyles, more or less lavish, that they ostensibly can afford.

The inherited system thus defines itself by the fact that what individuals understand as being in their interest and economic institutions are mutually reinforcing. On the one hand, therefore, the institutions can plausibly (and not without justification) present themselves as legitimized by the choices of the individual: just like the political choices of our democratic societies can be said to be grounded in the preferences expressed by the voters, the economic system responds, it may claim, to the sovereignty of the consumer (Galbraith 1973). On the other hand, the individual, as an economic agent, may believe, in good faith, that she has no choice: trapped, as producer of goods or services, in a system which favours generalized competition, and forced, as consumer, to support the comparison with others, she may well consider herself unable, on her own, to question the dominant production–consumption model. Of course, as citizen-voter, the individual does not face the same constraints: she may in principle opt for a different model, on the basis of a conception of the "good life" that is less dependent on market imperatives. But that individual still is faced with a limited set of political options to choose from, none of which (with few exceptions) proposes a genuine alternative to the quest for growth. Moreover, in the beauty contest for votes that political parties compete in in the hope of seducing the average voter, the programme that promises a constant improvement of material living conditions and the creation of a legal and economic order that favours an increase of consumption has one major advantage on its competitors: on its face at least, far from imposing on society one particular conception of the good life, such a programme allows each member of society to define his or her own ends, and economic prosperity, measured in monetary terms (as an increase in the wealth available), may be seen as simply a means towards fulfilling such ends, *whatever they may be*. Although it shapes our deepest perceptions of our representations of "success" and "happiness", the obsessive quest for growth can present itself as respecting the plurality of conceptions of the "good life": its ability to thus obfuscate the extent to which it restricts imagination is its most important ideological success.

Democracy: escaping the cage

This therefore is a very peculiar cage indeed. We have built it generation after generation: we therefore should be able to dismantle it, in order to escape from it. This however cannot be done by any single individual on his (or her) own: what is required is a collective action to be initiated, at societal scale. Moreover, and perhaps even more troubling, the citizen-voters and the economic agents seem, by their daily choices, to be satisfied with the status quo. It is understandable therefore that some, faced with such a predicament, call for authoritarian solutions at worst – this is the case for instance of Hans Jonas (Jonas 1979) – or at best, for scenarios that tend to impoverish democracy by giving a greater weight to experts or to enlightened technocrats. Dominique Bourg and Terry Whiteside, in this spirit, offer a vision of what might be called a "checks" democracy, by the establishment of a "higher chamber" specifically tasked with taking into account the interests of future generations (Bourg and Whiteside 2010).

Yet it is the opposite that is now required. Not the return of the Philosopher-Kings, but to anchor the state in society and society in the state. Not the emptying out of democracy in the name of the ecological emergency and of the "false consciousness" of the masses, whose minds are so hopelessly colonized by the dominant ideology, but the exact opposite: the radicalization of democracy, so that each individual may be allowed to better fulfil his or her *instituting* role: his or her role as norm creator, by the exercise of individual autonomy. Indeed, escaping the cage means for each individual the ability to challenge the social norms in the web of which he or she is caught: individual autonomy is only plausible if combined with collective autonomy, that is, with a questioning of the inherited norms and the conceptions of "success" or "happiness" that such norms embody.[2]

This is the first reason why the governance of transition in a post-growth society requires the creation of spaces in which the re-creation of norms by the individual should again become a real possibility. The classic forms of representative democracy and of responsible consumption shall not suffice. In our complex societies, characterized both by multilevel governance and by the lengthening of production chains – the result of a deepening of the division of labor – individuals can only bring about limited changes through the ballot and the wallet – as voters and as consumers, taking part in elections and acting as responsible purchasers of goods and services. The systems we inherit from are relatively inert: their various components (socio-technical, socio-economic and socio-cultural) have co-evolved, and now appear to be mutually reinforcing, resulting in significant obstacles to change (Geels 2011). Moreover, the responses from both the political system and markets – if they respond at all – both are relatively poor and come relatively late (for political systems, see Gilens 2012; Gilens and Page 2014). There is a risk therefore that, if we content ourselves with these two instruments of control, we lose the race against time which has now commenced: the ecosystems are being degraded, and the social links eroded, faster than the system can react.

Moreover, the signals coming from the ballot box or from the purchasing choices of consumers tend to be ambiguous, and they can easily be reinterpreted by the actors to whom they are addressed: such reinterpretation typically takes the form of a de-radicalization, or sometimes of a simple co-optation, as illustrated by the praise for various forms of "green growth" or the destiny of "fair trade". The evolution of the democratic system of representation is telling in this regard. In the standard understanding of representative democracy, the citizen-voter is the principal, and his or her representative is the agent: the principal (the voter) delegates certain powers to the agent (the elected representative) so as to ensure that the voter's preferences are fulfilled. In practice, however, the relationship is inverted: the representative ignores the wishes of the agent, and the world of political representatives is perceived as composed of elites, in the hands of technocrats or, even worse, captured by lobbies, instead of responding to the wishes of the population as a whole. Public choice theory provides in this regard a description of politics that is not without foundation (Buchanan and Tullock 1958; Stigler 1971), and should call for a reaction precisely from those, the believers in the strength of democracy, who are suspicious of its normative prescriptions.

The mystique of the labyrinth

There are escape routes. But it is the plural that matters. To escape, we first need to avoid seeing ourselves as if trapped in a labyrinth, in which there would be one single "correct" path to be followed. Instead of this fantasy of the One Right Solution, we should espouse the idea of the experimentalist search in many directions at the same time. And, instead of the uniformity of solutions, which the classical tools used by the state generally presupposes, we should welcome the idea of a patient quest for innovations that open the range of the possibilities.

Decentralizing the search for solutions

The revitalization of local democracy stimulates the search for new solutions: veto points are fewer at that level, and the possibilities of synergies between different policy areas are greater (McKibben 2007). Local democracy thus could favour overcoming the division between the "decision-makers" and the "decision-receivers", bringing the decision closer to the preoccupations of those in the name of whom it is adopted. Similarly, the strengthening of "civil society" (i.e. of the full range of associations in which individuals seek, on a voluntary basis, to build a collective action) allows each individual to build social links on the basis of shared convictions and of a common will for change, and thus to take part in collective actions. The point is not of course to favour a return to the communitarianisms of the past, in which the circumstances of birth led to replace the individual in his communities of origin, defining his role in the division of social labour as well as the solidarity mechanisms he or she could rely on through the "proximate protection" – from family members, from the community of neighbours, or from the profession he or she belonged to. The point is, rather, to allow each member of society an opportunity to co-construct with others certain alternatives, and thereby to invent new ways of life – new ways of moving, of eating, or of working – escaping from the standardization of modern society.

This utopia is already part of our daily experience. At the scale of the neighbourhood, of the school, or of the town, ordinary citizens permanently innovate. They invent new ways of sharing, rescuing a certain idea of the "commons" that was once thought to be definitely relegated to the past, after the loss of traditional forms of solidarity and the establishment of a hyper-individualistic society in which the position of each individual seems to be defined by his or her consumption. They put in place tools that allow a relocalization of economic relationships, breathing new life in local exchange systems and encouraging a reliance on local currencies to maximize the impacts on the local economy of market exchanges. In the areas of energy, of transport or of food, they encourage new ways of producing and of consuming. They score twice: they try to reduce their ecological footprint – often succeeding in doing so[3] – at the same time that they seek to strengthen the links between individuals, thus combating social exclusion (Dervojeda *et al.* 2013; AEIDL 2013).

In the setting up of these so-called "citizens' initiatives", the process matters as much as the end result. These initiatives aim, of course, at the "energy descent" (a concept initially coined by economists Odum and Odum in 2001 (Odum and Odum 2001: 4)), and at building more resilient local communities, better equipped to resist to shocks, whether economic or natural, by nurturing a diversity of local resources. But they also seek to affirm, at the micropolitical level of cultural practices and of social relationships, requirements of democracy and participation that elevate each individual, really, as the co-author of his or her environment. Autonomy should mean not only the capacity to shape alternatives, but also the ability to question the dominant representation of the motivations of actors.

Our societies seem to be unwilling to acknowledge the existence of individual motivations other than those that are purely economic in nature. Mainstream social science has proven its ability to reinterpret all individual behavior as animated by a hidden logic, which is that of individual utility maximization and of the economic calculus – such a calculus being at times described as corresponding to rationality itself, as in the economic science of Robbins or Becker or, more subtly, as in the work of Daniel Kahneman, who ends up defining such calculus as the only reasoning that is not victim of "bias" (Robbins 1932: 15; Becker 1992; Kahneman 2011). The full range of mechanisms that seek to guide society in a particular direction seem to be founded on this rather brute anthropology, this caricature of the human actor that economics textbooks capture as the "homo economicus": ultimately, it is this caricature, this "rational fool" in Sen's apt phrase (Sen 1977), that provides the foundations for both legal regulations and economic incentives. Yet, even a superficial glance at history or at societies different than our own would convince us that this motivation is just one episode, one moment in the evolution of human societies. It may be dominant here and now; it is neither eternally valid nor valid in all societies even today, and even in our societies, it does not rule entirely unchallenged.[4]

The learning state

The revitalization of local democracy and the strengthening of civil society and thus of the potential for citizen-led initiatives go hand in hand: such initiatives shall only be able to emerge, and be sustained, if they can be supported by hybrid governance mechanisms involving ordinary citizens, private economic actors and public authorities, in the design and the implementation of alternatives. However, just like we should avoid falling into the trap of thinking that society is made of a single cloth, so that change could only be conceived of as radical and as bringing about a complete replacement of one system by another, we should guard ourselves from the exact opposite illusion: local alternatives shall only have lasting impacts, and gradually spread across society, if they are supported (and their dissemination encouraged) by levels of governance that are not solely local.

At these higher levels of governance, what is needed therefore is a change in the dominant culture of governance. Since Plato's *Republic*, which placed its fate in the hands of the Philosopher-Kings and their expert wisdom, the task of Politics has traditionally been thought of as having to think for society, and to impose on society certain solutions, as it were, "from above". In such a scheme, it is almost inevitable that local diversity and the specificity of the contexts in which regulatory and policy frameworks are implemented shall be negated – eradicated if possible, or at least perceived as a problem to be overcome: after all, if a solution is deemed desirable because it is the most rational, or seen as the one that best serves the general interest, why should it not be generalized across society? It is this very scheme that we must now put into question, and it is this task of Politics that should now give way to another. For Politics should not be homogenizing per necessity. Instead, it could recast itself as serving local initiatives, thus allowing them to flourish by removing the constraints that are obstacles to their growth and dissemination. The role of higher levels of governance, in this view, should be to manage the externalities; to design the framework within which the local initiative develops so as to allow it to grow, by supporting what might be called "enabling mechanisms" – mechanisms which allow to support the diversity of social innovations by adapting the legal and economic institutions which facilitate their establishment and their further development; and finally, to accelerate collective learning, encouraging each local entity to gain from the experiments led by other local entities, both as a source of inspiration and as a means to enhance accountability.

Social innovations and collective learning

Local experimentation therefore is advantageous also for another reason, which has just been alluded to: it can be a searching device, and accelerate collective learning. The transition to a society that ranks other objectives (such as well-being, or real freedom understood as the expansion of its members' capabilities) above economic growth, shall not be effected all at once; nor shall it be achieved by relying only on the limited range of instruments – regulatory reforms or economic incentives – that the state may use. Social psychology has highlighted the limited impact of such instruments, which impose on individuals injunctions that rely on "extrinsic" motivations (Ryan and Deci 2000a, 2000b; Moller *et al.* 2006), and thus treat individuals like objects rather than as subjects of their own history (Arendt 1990 [1958]). Individuals on whom rules are imposed, to whom subsidies are promised, or who are threatened with having to pay taxes, will act in order to comply with the rule, to capture the subsidy, or to avoid paying the tax – but they will otherwise pursue their own life objectives, deviating as little as possible from such objectives that they have set for themselves. In contrast, behavioural changes that rely on the *intrinsic* motivations of the individual shall be resilient: because they are based on the individual's identity or self-image or on the values that the individual treats as his/her own, such changes will persist in time, even though the context (and the external incentives it provides) may have evolved. This is true, in particular, as regards pro-environmental behaviour (Lavergne *et al.* 2010). Moreover, as individuals seek to design solutions, in the immediate environment in which they operate, that may be responses to the ecological crisis (new ways of producing and of consuming, new lifestyles, new economic models), a form of democratic experimentalism emerges: a collective search commences, from which solutions may grow that can gradually result in new social norms solidifying, which shall be diffused from individual to individual before being generalized across society and replace existing routines.

This process is made possible by two properties of such social innovations. First, if such innovations are assessed by their ability to reduce our ecological footprint, and supported, where their contribution is seen as promising, by the establishment of enabling mechanisms at higher levels of governance, such solutions also may be seen as public goods: they are a new source of knowledge about the escape routes from the current ecological impasse, which society as a whole may benefit from. Social innovators are searchers, and the knowledge base they contribute to build is a positive externality, a by-product of their solitary quest for solutions.

Second, social innovations that have been successfully experimented in some settings have an empowering effect on others: others, operating in other settings or in other jurisdictions, can more easily demand from decision-makers that they take such experiments into account, and that they create the legal and economic institutions that may favour their emergence. Of course, proposing to create "spontaneous", "citizen-led" social innovations by operating from above, is about as contradictory as proposing to fasten the growth of a tree by pulling on its branches: ultimately, if there is no appetite for the social innovation in question, encouraging its diffusion shall lead, at best, to temporary changes on a limited scale. However, the establishment of "enabling mechanisms" for such innovations, together with a deliberate attempt to learn from what has worked elsewhere, can stimulate reflexivity within a given community. Innovations that have succeeded elsewhere are discussed. Routines are disrupted. The community is put in motion, as its members start to question the dominant lifestyles and to realize that other ways of relating to one another and to Nature may be more desirable than the agonistic and atomistic understanding of the Self that economic science has imposed on us. New questions arise also about the responsibility of the decision-makers in the process of change: are they doing enough to favour the emergence of social innovations? Each member of the community is forced to ask him- or herself: is there any role I should play in these social innovations that are now creating a wider range of alternatives for me to choose from?

Social learning and reflexivity

By this networking of local experiments, a form of learning commences as the established routines within each community are interrogated, in the light of the experience of the other communities. This represents a gain in reflexivity for each entity. Following Kuhn and others (Kuhn 1962; Argyris 1974; Argyris and Schön 1978), we may distinguish here different levels of learning. To learn, is first to correct mistakes or to fill in blindspots in the paradigm under which one is working. The working hypothesis remains unchanged: experience leads to amend the hypothesis on certain points, without the hypothesis being more fundamentally questioned. Kuhn would say that "normal" science may continue. Argyris would add: first-order learning has occurred, which consists not in revising one's framework of analysis or in redefining one's objectives, but in opting for different means, better suited perhaps to achieve the objective that one is pursuing. It may occur however that a deeper revision is required. In the light of the experience gained, the dominant paradigm cannot be maintained: a paradigm change is required, which Kuhn calls a scientific "revolution". This is second-order learning. In this type of learning, however, while the working hypothesis may have to be amended – or while we may have to opt for different objectives – we still do not question our very identity, that is, the representation we have of our interest. But we can move further, to a form of learning that leads to question that representation itself, in other terms, to redefine one's very identity – whom we are, and what we want. This requires a genealogical *démarche*, in which we ask where the received understandings of "progress" or of "success" originate from at the level of the individual or of society: it is not just that the means are inadequate for the attainment of certain ends, and it is not just that the ends are inadequately defined – rather, it is our deeper beliefs about what is desirable that are challenged, our representation of ourselves that is transformed (Swieringa and Wierdsma 1992; Peschl 2008).

In order to move towards a society that escapes the trap of growth, it is such a third-order learning that is required. The capitalist and productivist system on the one hand, the individual who is both its co-author and its addressee on the other, mutually support each other. Just like the *homo economicus* is not simply a "product" of capitalist culture, capitalist culture is not just a "creation" of the *homo economicus*: "There is always homology and deep correspondance between the structure of the personality and the content of the culture, and there is no reason to predetermine the one by the other" (Castoriadis 1975: 41). In response to this circularity and to the phenomenon of mutual reinforcement that it leads to, the transition calls for a gain in reflexivity: we need to revisit the fundamental question of how each individual defines his or her understanding of the "good life", and at the societal level, the question of the trajectory that we wish to pursue collectively.

To provide a narrative that people may relate to, may constitute an important role of governments. Indeed, this is one key function of planning, not in the meaning of five-year plans deciding on the allocation of resources and setting binding targets as in the Soviet era, but in the meaning of providing a general orientation, offering to economic actors as well as to citizens a relatively stable and predictable framework, a broad vision for the future, allowing each member of society to see him- or herself as contributing to change at the collective level (Dupuy 2012). The challenge here is to provide a narrative that stimulates social innovation, but that does not restrict the imagination of the actors. Although good practices may be identified and highlighted, and although they may constitute a source of inspiration, generalization of such practices immediately makes us run the risk of homogenization and standardization, which would mean the end of progress, as the permanent search for new solutions would come to an end (Lévi-Strauss 2007 [1952]).

Conclusion

At the individual level, the requirement of autonomy is a requirement that each actor defines his or her own understanding of happiness, without such understanding being imposed by the injunctions of the consumer society. At the societal level, it is the ability for each society to define its own historical trajectory. The "always more" seems more plausible than ever as producers gain in efficiency under the pressure of competition, as workers constantly improve their productivity in part because of the incentives of financial rewards, and as consumers consume. But the immature idea of an infinite progress, of unlimited growth on a limited planet on which we depend both for the resources we extract from it and for the waste we dump on it – this idea now must face the wall of ecological boundaries. Escaping the cage that we have built around us is more urgent than ever. We can succeed. We shall succeed, however, only if we recognize the potential of social innovations that prepare the transition, and if we favour their emergence and their dissemination. Only then, shall the lock finally be broken.

Notes

1 This failure of the imagination is connected to what Scitovsky identifies, with his usual lucidity, as a major liability of advanced societies: boredom, as a result of the inability of individuals to occupy their time in other ways than by producing or consuming (Scitovsky 1976). André Gorz noted that we have invested in technologies that allow us to save time, but that we are ill-equipped to use all the time that has been freed up. Boundless consumption becomes a substitute to this lack of imagination: as Keynes already remarked in a conference of 1928, "we have been too long trained to pay and not to enjoy" (Keynes 1972 [1930]).

2 It is for this reason that the proposal to align production and consumption on the needs of the community concerned, rather than on the expectations of the shareholders of the providers of goods or services or on the quest for GDP growth which so obsesses the state, is so deeply subversive politically. For such a proposal supposes that those who produce and those who consume meet, to decide for themselves, in particular, which are the limits that should not be crossed (Gorz 1980: 178). It is only through such democratic processes, allowing truly autonomous choices to be made (communities deciding what they want, collectively), that we can hope to remain within the limits of the planetary boundaries that scientists have defined (Rockström *et al.* 2009; Steffen *et al.* 2015).

3 There are exceptions. An important literature now questions the idea that reducing the geographical distance between producers and consumers, for instance by establishing so-called "short food chains", has a positive impact on the environment (Schmidt 2009; Foodmetres 2014). Similarly, the "sharing economy" may lead to certain forms of hyperconsumption and accelerate the obsolescence of the tools or items that are shared, as well as leading to an increase in the number of short distances travelled by these objects (Demailly and Novel 2014).

4 As noted by Castoriadis, the types of motivation (and the corresponding values that polarize and orientation the lives of human beings) are social creations: "each culture institutes values of its own and tame individuals in accordance with such values" (Castoriadis 1975: 37, our translation).

References

AEIDL (European Association of Local Development Initiatives/Association européenne des initiatives de développement local) (2013). *Europe in Transition: Local Communities Leading the Way to a Low-carbon Society.*

Arendt, H. (1990 [1958]). *On Revolution.* London: Penguin.

Argyris, C. (1974). Single-Loop and Double-Loop Models in Research on Decision Making. *Administrative Science Quarterly*, 21(3): 363–375.

Argyris, C. and Schön, D. (1978). *Organizational Learning: A Theory of Action Perspective.* Reading, MA: Addison-Wesley.

Becker, G. (1992). *The Economic Way of Looking at Life.* Nobel Lecture in Economics.

Berman, H.J. (1983). *Law and Revolution II: The Impact of the Protestant Reformations on the Western Legal Tradition.* Cambridge, MA: Harvard University Press (trans. from A. Wijffels (2011) *Droit et révolution. L'impact des réformes protestantes sur la tradition juridique occidentale*, Paris: Fayard).

Bourg, D. and Whiteside, K. (2010). *Vers une démocratie écologique. Le citoyen, le savant et le politique.* Paris: Seuil.

Buchanan, J. and Tullock, G. (1958). *The Calculus of Consent: Logical Foundations of Constitutional Democracy.* Indianapolis: Liberty Fund.

Cassiers, I. (ed.) (2015). *Redefining Prosperity.* London: Routledge.

Castoriadis, C. (1975). *L'institution imaginaire de la société*. Paris: Seuil.

Daly, H. (1996). *Beyond Growth: The Economics of Sustainable Development*. Boston: Beacon Press.

De Schutter, O. (2015). Welfare State Reform and Social Rights. *Netherlands Quarterly of Human Rights*, 33(2): 123–162.

Demailly, D. and Novel, A.-S. (2014). *Economie du partage: enjeux et opportunités pour la transition écologique*. IDDRI Study no. 3/14. Paris: Institut du développement durable et des relations internationales.

Dervojeda, K., Verzijl, D., Nagtegaal, F., Lengton, M., Elco Rouwmaat, E., Monfardini, E. and Frideres, L. (2013). The Sharing Economy. Accessibility Based Business Models for Peer-to-Peer Markets. Business Innovation Observatory. Case Study 12. European Commission, DG Enterprise and Industry, Brussels.

Dolan, P., Peasgood, T. and White, M. (2008). Do We Really Know What Makes Us Happy? A Review of the Economic Literature on the Factors Associated With Subjective Well-Being. *Journal of Economic Psychology*, 29: 94–122.

Dupuy, J.-P. (2012). *L'avenir de l'économie. Sortir de l'écomystification*. Paris: Flammarion.

Foodmetres (2014). Metropolitan Footprint Analysis and Sustainability Impact Assessment of Short Food Chain Scenarios. (Part D5.1 of the project). Available online at: www.foodmetres.eu/.

Galbraith, J.K. (1973). *Economics and the Public Purpose*. Boston: Houghton Mifflin Company.

Geels, F.W. (2011). The Multi-Level Perspective on Sustainability Transitions: Responses to Seven Criticisms. *Environmental Innovations and Societal Transformations*, 1: 24–40.

Gilens, M. (2012). *Affluence & Influence: Economic Inequality and Political Power in America*. Princeton: Princeton University Press.

Gilens, M. and Page, B. (2014). Testing Theories of American Politics: Elites, Interest Groups and Average Citizens. *Perspectives on Politics*, 12(3): 564–581.

Gorz, A. (1980). *Adieux au prolétariat*. Paris: Galilée.

Jonas, H. (1979). *Le principe responsabilité, une éthique pour la civilisation technologique*. Paris: Cerf.

Kahneman, D. (2011). *Thinking, Fast and Slow*. New York: Farrar, Straus and Giroux.

Keynes, J.M. (1972 [1930]). Economic Possibilities for Our Grandchildren. In *Essays in Persuasion*, vol. 9. In Donald Moggridge (ed.), *Collected Writings of John Maynard Keynes*. London: Macmillan, pp. 321–331.

Kuhn, T. (1962). *The Structure of Scientific Revolutions*. Chicago: University of Chicago Press.

Laval, C. (2007). *L'homme économique. Essai sur les racines du néolibéralisme*. Paris: Gallimard.

Lavergne, K.J., Sharp, E., Pelletier, L.G. and Holtby, A. (2010). The Role of Perceived Government Style in the Facilitation of Self-Determined and Non Self-Determined Motivation for Pro-Environmental Behavior. *Journal of Environmental Psychology*, 30(2): 169–177.

Layard, R. (2005). *Happiness: Lessons from a New Science*. London: Allen Lane.

Lévi-Strauss, C. (2007 [1952]). *Race et histoire*. Paris: Gallimard.

McKibben, B. (2007). *Deep Economy: The Wealth of Communities and the Durable Future*. New York: Henry Holt & Co.

Méda, D. (2013). *La mystique de la croissance*. Paris: Flammarion.

Moller, A.C., Ryan, R.M. and Deci, E. (2006). Self-Determination Theory and Public Policy: Improving the Quality of Consumer Decisions Without Using Coercion. *Journal of Public Policy and Marketing*, 25(1): 104–116.

Odum H.T. and Odum, E.C. (2001). *A Prosperous Way Down*. Boulder: University Press of Colorado.

Peschl, M.F. (2008). Triple-Loop Learning as Foundation for Profound Change, Individual Cultivation, and Radical Innovation: Construction Processes Beyond Scientific and Rational Knowledge. *Munich Personal RePEc Archive*, No. 9940.

Robbins, L. (1932). *An Essay on the Nature and Significance of Economic Science*. London: Macmillan.

Rockström, J., Steffen, W., Noone, K., Persson, Å., Chapin III, F.S., Lambin, E., Lenton, T.M., Scheffer, M., Folke, C., Schellnhuber, H.J., Nykvist, B., de Wit, C.A., Hughes, T., van der Leeuw, S., Rodhe, H., Sörlin, S., Snyder, P.K., Costanza, R., Svedin, U., Falkenmark, M., Karlberg, L., Corell, R.W., Fabry, V.J., Hansen, J., Walker, B., Liverman, D., Richardson, K., Crutzen, P. and Foley, J. (2009). Planetary Boundaries: Exploring the Safe Operating Space for Humanity. *Ecology and Society*, 14(2): 32.

Ryan, R. and Deci, E. (2000a). Intrinsic and Extrinsic Motivations: Classic Definitions and New Directions. *Contemporary Educational Psychology*, 25: 54–67.

Ryan, R. and Deci, E. (2000b). Self-Determination Theory and the Facilitation of Intrinsic Motivation, Social Development, and Well-Being. *American Psychologist*, 55(1): 68–78.

Schmidt, H.-J. (2009). Carbon Footprinting, Labelling and Life Cycle Assessment. *The International Journal of Life Cycle Assessment*, 14(S1): 6–9.

Scitovsky, T. (1976). *The Joyless Economy: The Psychology of Human Satisfaction*. Oxford and New York: Oxford University Press (1992 revised edition).

Sen, A.K. (1977). Rational Fools: A Critique of the Behavioral Foundations of Economic Theory. *Philosophy & Public Affairs*, 6(4): 317–344.

Steffen, W., Richardson, K., Rockström, J., Cornell, S.E., Fetzer, I., Bennett, E.M., Biggs, R., Carpenter, S.R., de Vries, W., de Wit, C., Folke, C., Gerten, D., Heinke, J., Mace, G.M., Persson, L.M., Ramanathan, V., Reyers, B. and Sörlin, S. (2015). Planetary Boundaries: Guiding Human Development on a Changing Planet. *Science*, 347(6223). doi:10.1126/science.1259855.

Stigler, G.J. (1971). The Theory of Economic Regulation. *The Bell Journal of Economics and Management Science*, 2(1): 3–21.

Swieringa, J. and Wierdsma, A. (1992). *Becoming a Learning Organization*. Reading, MA: Addison-Wesley.

Tawney, R. (1920). *The Acquisitive Society*. New York: Harcourt Brace and Howe.

Veblen, T. (1899). *The Theory of the Leisure Class: An Economic Study of Institutions*. New York: Macmillan (1994 edition, New York: Dover).

Weber, M. (1992 [1930]). *The Protestant Ethic and the Spirit of Capitalism*. London and New York: Routledge.

Weber, M. (2005 [1927]). *General Economic History*. New Brunswick and London: Transaction Publishers.

For Product Safety Concerns and Information please contact our EU
representative GPSR@taylorandfrancis.com
Taylor & Francis Verlag GmbH, Kaufingerstraße 24, 80331 München, Germany

www.ingramcontent.com/pod-product-compliance
Ingram Content Group UK Ltd.
Pitfield, Milton Keynes, MK11 3LW, UK
UKHW020945180425
457613UK00019B/534